LEADERSHIP
that LASTS

LEADERSHIP
that LASTS

SEVEN ACTIONS TOWARD
AN ENDURING IMPACT

———

TIM MATHENEY

SPIRE LEADERSHIP GROUP
PHILADELPHIA

In memory of my parents,

Bettie and Dean Matheney

who taught me about lasting values
and encouraged me to become a leader.

CONTENTS

CHAPTER ONE

THE FIRST LEADER

In the mid-1950s, a Midwestern mother shook her teenaged son awake in the middle of the night.

Through the fog of sleep, he heard, "Dean, you have to go get your dad."

It took only a quick glance at his alarm clock for the boy to realize the reason. It had happened dozens of times.

His eyes still closed, he told his mother, "Okay. I'll go."

He crawled from the warmth of his bed and felt the night chill. He threw on his coat and glanced in his little brother's room on the way out. Good, he thought, he's still asleep.

He trudged the several blocks to his dad's favorite haunt, the aptly-named Caboose Club, where conductors, engineers, and clerks in this railroad town went to escape their troubles.

When the boy, known throughout the small town for strikeouts and no-hitters, entered the musty, dark bar, the man behind the counter greeted him familiarly, "Your dad's over there."

It wasn't unusual for the bartender to see the boy at that time of the night – or early morning. The son walked over to his slumping father, who steadied himself on the bar railing with weathered hands from a hard life of work on the railroad.

"I'm not ready to go yet," the drunken man barked as coherently as he could muster, his breath toxic from whiskey and beer.

"Yes, you are. Time to go." The healthy, athletic boy lifted his father from the bar stool and held him firm as the man lost his balance. The son raised his father's arm around his shoulders, and the two began their short journey home.

It was early morning, so fortunately there were few people on the streets. But an occasional car would pass, its headlights illuminating the identities of the pair. Humiliation, sadness, and anger filled the boy.

After climbing the front steps of their home, the son passed his father, who looked much older than his years, to his mother who by that time had been numbed by this frequent routine. The boy walked quietly to his room, trying not to wake his little brother, but knowing his father's incoherent babble probably would – again.

In his room, the boy took off his jacket, folded it neatly on a chair, and collapsed in bed. His mind struggled to return to sleep – the demands of tomorrow looming over him, the smell of his father's breath, and the look on his mother's face replaying in his mind like a record.

More than 50 years had passed since the last time the boy, now an old man, had to retrieve his father from the bar. It was early spring, 2016, and warmth, happiness, and laughter filled his new home in south Florida despite his very real fears about the day ahead. Just a few moments before, the man's younger son had set his computer on his dad's lap, hit a few buttons, and set up a video conversation with family gathered in his granddaughter's hospital room in Ohio. The man marveled at the clear image of his first great-grandchild. The baby had been born six days before the man's 80th birthday. It was the first time the great-grandfather had seen the baby. He chatted with his beaming grandchildren gathered in the hospital room and, hearing the newborn gurgle, the man released a hearty, contented laugh.

As he watched his granddaughter cradle her son, the man thought of the moment he became a father for the first time, holding his newborn son. He also remembered moments decades earlier when roles were reversed, and he had to embrace his drunken father as he tumbled from a barstool.

The loving presence of his son at the condo, the vision of his great-grandson, the affection he always felt from family – they all confirmed for the old man that the choices he made were nothing like his father's.

Early the following morning, the old man was prepped for cardiac surgery with three major procedures ahead of him. He told a nurse, "I have a lot to live for. I got to see my first great-grandchild *on the computer* last night. Unbelievable!"

"We FaceTimed," his son added. The nurse nodded and smiled at the sweet old man.

With preparations for his operation and the first injections of sedatives complete, the nurses wheeled the man toward the surgery room.

His son said, "Love you, Dad," and the old man's brother added, "Dean, we'll see you after surgery. You're going to be fine." As they wheeled him forward, the man, with the drugs hitting his arteries, grinned at a nurse and told her how pretty she was. "But I know I'm too old for you," and he smiled. The nurse gently patted the old man's hand.

Hours later I was finally able to see my father again in the Intensive Care Unit, my partner Ken at my side. The surgery on my father's deteriorating heart had not gone well. His left ventricle had failed, and it was only the myriad of machines attended by kind technicians and nurses that were keeping him alive. His face was bloated and discolored by the effects of medications, the surgery, and the machines that kept his blood flowing.

As a child, I watched the man now kept alive by machines leave for work as an assistant principal, with his shoes shined and his pants smartly pressed. I saw the respect in other people's eyes when he read passages from the Bible and distributed Communion alongside the pastor at our small-town Methodist church. I admired the patches and medals he earned from commanding his university's ROTC unit. And I read the commendations he received during his brief active duty in the Army with great pride.

To me, he was *the first leader.*

In the couple of days that followed my dad's surgery, I managed to hold myself together despite knowing the difficult decision that we faced. I talked with my brother, Steve, on the phone often. He was supportive and involved as best as he could, but he was in Ohio doing what he should have been doing at that moment – attending to his daughter and his first-born grandchild. Steve talked to my dad's nurses directly and was as knowledgeable about my dad's condition as I was.

My uncle, too, helped think through the situation, always respecting that any decision about my Dad was ours as his sons.

Knowing that my father would never recover, my brother and I agreed on the course of action.

On the morning of my father's 80th birthday, after ICU nurses sang "Happy Birthday" to him, my partner and I were once again at his side. I held his hand, kissed his forehead, and told him that he had been a very good father. He was a gentle, kind man with a playful sense of humor. He provided well for his family and was a devoted husband to Mom. He never, ever needed to be dragged home from a bar, drunk.

My first leader.

As I stood next to my father's bed, my mind raced as I thought about how my father had inspired me to be as good of a man and a leader as I could be. I had graduated from Princeton with honors thanks to the sacrifices of my very middle-class parents. I had triumphed over "the closet" in my 20s and became a strong, confident, well-adjusted gay man. I had become a respected high school teacher and years later the principal of a well-regarded high school, responsible for the education of nearly 3,000 young people. I hoped I had done those things with the thoughtfulness and intelligence of the man lying in the hospital bed.

Often with the voice of my father in my head, I had made millions of decisions in the leadership roles I've held since I was a teenager, but none like the one I made that day in the ICU on March 7, 2016. My brother and I knew what Dad would want us to do.

When the nurses and technicians turned off the machines, they stepped to the edge of the room, leaving Ken and me at his side. Dad's heart stopped beating immediately, and he passed quietly. I cried with deep heaves of sadness for a couple of minutes, Ken holding me firmly. Several nurses wept, too. I soon gathered myself, just as my father would have, and we left the ICU.

Losing my father, I realized with time, had changed me. Anyone who has had to make a decision about the end of a parent's life understands this.

I thought about the implications of no longer being someone's child. I had made the ultimate decision about the father I loved and admired. Nothing else would ever hold the gravity of what I had to do that day. After that decision, I felt a new kind of strength. A more resilient confidence.

In the months after my dad's death, I also felt a growing impatience in me. I was impatient with relationships that didn't contribute positively to my life. I felt the urge to invest more deeply in those people who nurtured my spirit.

I was also increasingly impatient with one of my most characteristic traits. I had always been a pleaser by nature. As a child I was always eager to please my parents and my teachers, and that trait had continued into adulthood. But now, pleasing others just for the sake of pleasing had lost its appeal. I knew I needed to break free from the burden of accepting responsibility for others' happiness.

Losing my father also had a second significant impact. Seeing my father's frailty from the days before surgery to his last breath helped me accept my own vulnerability. As I applied lotion on his bare back the night before surgery, his weakness was tangible. Seeing my father so fragile was so different from how I had always thought of him.

As he lay motionless in his hospital bed, I realized in a way I'd never really known before how finite our lives are. Losing my mother was very different. She had been ill for several years, and her passing represented a moment of grace. But my father's death reminded me how limited our lives are. My days are finite. I can't postpone my dreams.

Changed by my father's death and inspired by his life, I chose to leave a great job, start my own company, and pursue my passions. With this book, honoring everything my first leader taught me, I'm pleased to follow a dream and share with you lessons from my career in leadership.

CHAPTER TWO

CONCEPTIONS
OF LEADERSHIP

I'll be honest with you. I'm concerned about leadership.

I'm concerned about leaders who
... favor self-aggrandizement over timeless principles.
... cater to our basest instincts of fear and insecurity.
... say anything in order to hear the sound of applause.
... devalue the expertise and hard work of people who serve
   them.

I'm also concerned about supposed leadership gurus who
... seek to convince audiences that leadership is easy.
... believe that the secrets to leadership can be found in catchy
   acronyms.
... try to teach about leadership without having extensive
   experience as a leader.
... claim that answers to all of the problems of leadership can
   be contained between the front and back covers of a
   single book.

I don't.

Leading others, as most of us know, is puzzling, frustrating,
exhausting, and discouraging.

Leadership is hard. But it's also incredibly rewarding, and I
feel truly privileged to have had so many opportunities to lead.

In sharp contrast to authors who claim they have the secret
recipe to leadership is this book's conception of leadership.
Leadership that Lasts is about seven complex actions, each profiled in
a chapter, that effective leaders take in order to make an enduring
impact. They are, in summary . . .

Connect. Nurture relationships where others enrich your leadership and you enrich the lives of others.

Commit. Build your leadership on bedrock ethics and convictions.

Persevere. Develop resilience and lead around and through obstacles.

Thrive. Pursue wellness of the mind, body, and spirit.

Discover. Learn relentlessly and listen diligently for understanding.

Imagine. Envision individual and organizational excellence.

Dare. Practice authenticity and take the right kind of risks.

Each chapter introduces you to the people, ideas, and the personal experiences that have shaped my leadership. I hope that each chapter leads you to consider your leadership through each lens that I frame. The stories and concepts are intended to provoke reflection, not sell you a formula that, in the end, proves inadequate for the complex challenges of leadership.

The chapters of *Leadership that Lasts* draw on a diverse set of sources: business, military, psychology, sports, the arts, and, particularly, education. As you encounter some of my influences, I hope you'll become intrigued enough to explore further. I encourage you take the opportunity to watch videos of the All Blacks' *haka* or music of the P.S. 22 Chorus. Perhaps you'll want to explore design thinking or learn more about the Philadelphia Academy of School Leaders. Maybe you'll take a moment to think about the relationship between authenticity and vulnerability as they relate to your own leadership. I hope what you read in these pages is just the beginning of some productive detours on your current journey as a leader.

As you read *Leadership that Lasts*, you'll note a number of stories from my professional life. Out of respect for some people in the stories, I've used pseudonyms or avoided using names altogether. In a couple of cases, I've changed some minor details to protect the confidentiality of those involved, while preserving the key points of the anecdote.

My personal accounts, particularly from my years as a principal, are based on thick folders of artifacts I accumulated during that time. Knowing that I might want to write this book someday, I kept a file cleverly-labeled "The Book" into which I'd toss a document here and there. Newspaper clippings, printed copies of emails, and speeches brought back memories of a formative period in my leadership career. In my professional roles after the principalship, I regularly kept track of my work in notebooks, and I held onto all of them. They also were helpful in refreshing my recollections.

For other portions of the book, I've mentioned my sources within the text or have included them in "Acknowledgments and References" in the back of the book.

As you read I hope you'll consider sharing your own lessons of leadership by emailing me at tim@spireleadershipgroup.com. I would enjoy hearing about the people and ideas that've influenced your leadership. I'm eager to learn from you.

As you continue reading, I want you to know that I'm deeply grateful that you're sharing your most precious resource with me: time. I feel privileged to spend a few hours with you, and I wish you all the best as you **connect** deeply with those who enrich your life**, commit** to the right values, **persevere** through obstacles, **thrive** personally and professionally, constantly explore, **discover**, and **imagine** new possibilities**,** and **dare** to be audacious. Enjoy the journey.

CHAPTER THREE

CONNECT

As most of South Brunswick Township, in central New Jersey, slumbered in the early hours of December 20, 2004, two teenaged boys made their plans. One of them, an unlicensed 16-year-old, took his mother's car keys while she slept and drove over to pick up his friend. Before heading to the car, the younger boy quickly typed an away message in his instant messenger, then he joined his friend. Together they hit the streets of the silent community.

A few hours later, the first wave of commuters from the township scraped the frost from their windshields and began their 50-mile journey to Manhattan. As they headed toward the entrance of the turnpike, they pumped on their brakes as they approached the corner of Route 1 and Deans Lane. The lights of a host of emergency vehicles lit up the intersection. The presence of flashing lights on busy Route 1 wasn't at all unusual, but this early?

As the early bird commuters began their journeys, I was getting ready for school dodging gift boxes and wrapping paper. My cat nibbled on the green and red ribbon I had left out the night before. In less than a week, I'd be enjoying laughter and Christmas cookies in front of the fireplace at my parents' cozy home in northwestern Ohio.

I looked forward to the stretch of days away from school. It had been a demanding few months for this rookie principal of South Brunswick High School (SBHS), one of the largest schools in the state. I was still in my thirties and relatively inexperienced, with only three years as an assistant principal at a smaller school under my belt. The job was truly demanding – much had to be done to repair the damage caused by rapid enrollment growth and leadership instability. Three principals had served the school in the five most recent years – five principals in seven years.

My morning's preparations complete, I turned off the radio tuned to Christmas music and placed some files in my messenger bag.

My phone rang.

If a principal's phone rings 45 minutes before the school day starts, it's never good news. My boss's name, Gary McCartney, the Superintendent, appeared on the phone, and I flipped it open immediately, eager to know what was going on.

"Gary, what's up?" I answered.

There's been a bad accident in town. It looks like a couple of your kids were in it. The police said it looks really bad. I don't know much more, but the Chief said somebody would fill us in once they have an update."

Gary was unfailingly cool under pressure, but I could tell even he was shaken by the news.

"Oh, god. Was anyone killed? Any names?"

I didn't want to ask the question. I didn't want to know the answer. But I *had* to know. I was the principal, and I had to start preparing myself for the next few hours – days – weeks.

"No details yet. He just said it was bad. Really bad. So I'm expecting the worst," Gary responded.

"Okay, I'm leaving for school right now. I'll check up on things there and give you a call."

I hung up the call and jumped in the car for the short ride to school. As I drove, I thought about how to prepare a response to the horrific news. I would need to make sure the assistant principals were informed. As soon as students were in class, I would convene the school's Crisis Team. I'd also have to make sure Gary approved of the communications I'd share with staff members, students, parents, and the public. I expected a day that would demand all of my skills as a leader.

As I made my brief trip, school buses and commuters passing the scene of the crash gawked at the wreckage of a Ford Taurus. One half of the vehicle was wrapped around a telephone pole on the southbound side, with the other part lying 150 yards away. The car had been shredded in half by the force of the collision. Black tarps were stretched over the portion of the car that encircled the pole.

Fifteen minutes after I hung up with the Superintendent, I arrived at school. It was about 7 a.m., a half hour before classes started for the day. As students and teachers began to pass through the doors, I heard chatter about "a really bad accident on Route 1." I walked the halls, trying to assess the level of anxiety among teachers and students and to see if I could learn anything from their accounts.

Soon the bell reminding students to get to class rang, and a police sergeant came through the front doors of the school. Obviously agitated, he asked to speak to me in my office.

The horrific collision that morning, he told me, had involved two of our students, one of whom was dead with the other in serious condition at the hospital. I could feel my heart beat harder as he explained that they couldn't yet confirm the students' identities but they had a pretty good idea who they were. He shared the students' names. Even though I had only been at the school a few months I recognized both names and knew one student, a gregarious, fun-loving sophomore. "There's more," he said. "We found a note in one of the boy's pockets. We don't think it was an accident."

Traumatic situations weren't new to me. I had dealt with them before as a teacher and assistant principal, but this was unlike anything I had encountered. I composed myself and got as much information as I could from the police officer, relayed what I knew to the Superintendent, and started to gather key members of our staff who would be my important partners in the coming weeks.

After meeting with Assistant Principals and counselors, we decided that I'd hold off on making any announcements. From dealing with crisis situations in the past I knew that any initial information I received could be inaccurate. We also wanted to give the police the time they needed to communicate with the families who were affected. The team and I decided that I'd make an announcement later that morning, once our information was more solid, that shared that two students were involved in a serious car crash. I wouldn't mention the names of the students at that point. I would just reassure students and staff that I'd keep them informed and remind students that they could see their guidance counselors if they were concerned or upset.

At the time of this incident, cell phones were not a ubiquitous part of teenagers' lives. Rumors in crises like this flew a bit more slowly than they do now. Nevertheless, those with mobile phones began to receive text messages about the morning's tragedy. In a town like South Brunswick, everyone is only one or two degrees of separation from a police officer or firefighter. So information spread quickly on the identities of the boys in the vehicle.

As information, some right and some wrong, started to circulate over the course of the morning, I knew I had to make some type of announcement to reassure the school. Almost three hours into the school day – seven hours after the crash – this is what I said:

> "Teachers, please pardon this interruption. This is Mr. Matheney with a brief announcement. As you may have heard, two of our students were involved in a serious car accident very early this morning. I have been in regular communication with the South Brunswick Police throughout the day, and at this time the police have not released any official information about the incident. We want to share as much information with the school community about this situation as we can, and we will do so after we learn more from the police and the parents of the students involved.
>
> Students, if you would like to speak to a counselor about any emotions you're experiencing today, we will have a number of counselors in the library for the rest of the day. Finally, this announcement is for teachers: We will have a faculty meeting in the auditorium this afternoon immediately following the school day. Thank you."

As the day progressed, I made a point to walk the halls and check in with our counselors regularly. The police, after notifying the parents of the students and giving time for them to share the information among their families, provided me with formal confirmation that two SBHS students had been involved in the crash. One, 15 years old, had been killed, though they weren't officially releasing his name, and the other, 16, was hospitalized. The police confirmed for me that a suicide note was found in one boy's pocket, and there was evidence that the crash resulted from a suicide pact between the boys.

After consulting again with the Superintendent and the Crisis Team, I wrote a second announcement – intentionally using the term "accident" – that began,

"This is Mr. Matheney with further news about the accident this morning. We have been able to confirm through the police and the parents of the students involved that one of the two students in the car accident is currently hospitalized because of the injuries he suffered in the accident. The second student in the vehicle, I'm very sad to report, was pronounced dead at the scene. I just spoke to the Police Department, and at this time they are not confirming the student's name pending official identification.

In light of this sad news, I would ask that we observe a brief moment of silence."

I paused.

"I will make further announcements with more details as they become available.

Tomorrow we will continue with classes, but we will have counselors available in the library throughout the day and after school. Please do not hesitate to see them with any concerns or simply to take a moment to share the feelings you're experiencing.

I will be outside the main office after school if you have any further questions. Thank you."

By late afternoon, the media had picked up the story. Superintendent Gary McCartney and I decided to err on the side of communicating as openly as we could – especially in sharing how the school and district were responding to the tragedy. By 4:30 p.m. that day, journalists began to stream through my office for a statement. Reporters I recognized from the NBC, CBS and Fox New York affiliates posed questions to me on camera in my outer office. They were, I was surprised to find, largely deferential and kind. Nearly all introduced themselves by first expressing sympathies. Everyone is touched when a teenager's life is lost.

In the days that followed, a number of newspapers outside of New Jersey picked up the Associated Press account. *The New York Times*, *New York Post*, and the *Philadelphia Inquirer* wrote their own stories, highlighting the angle of the suicide pact. A few articles shared the message that one boy posted on his instant messenger before he left home in the Ford Taurus: "Sorry I can't be around for the holidays. Hopefully you can enjoy it without me."

As we dealt with the aftermath of the incident, I leaned heavily on the school's assistant principals and Crisis Team, and they performed admirably. At my side, advising me and leading the Crisis Team, was Sue Coyle, a senior member of the faculty who was a Student Assistance Counselor at the time. She ensured that the right people were in touch with the students' families and that the students and teachers affected most received extra attention. Our mutual respect and friendship was forged in those awful days.

As the week progressed, I saw different expressions of grief. There were students who were close to the boys and their families and felt a deep loss. There were students who had suffered their own traumas. The tragedy triggered the resurfacing of many emotions for them.

As we cared for students and staff in the days that followed, the school received a second major blow that same difficult week. As the school community mourned, veteran Assistant Principal Joe Valenti became seriously ill. Joe was my "right hand," functioning as the school's chief operating officer. In a coma with multiple organs near failure, Joe's condition was precarious for weeks. His illness was particularly hard on the faculty. A father figure for many, he was the glue that held the school together during its numerous leadership transitions. He had started at SBHS as a math teacher and spent his entire career serving the school. As our teachers prepared to attend a student's funeral, Joe was lying in the intensive care unit. In the weeks that followed, we weren't sure he would survive.

Two days before Christmas 2004, I entered the largest funeral home in the area to pay respects to the family who had lost a son and brother. I told them how sorry I was – how I would remember the spirited boy with a goofy sense of humor. As I left the funeral home, a long line of students, families, and staff members wound around the building. Numb from the week's events, I got into my car loaded with Christmas gifts for my family and began the long drive home to my family in Ohio.

MOVING FORWARD TOGETHER

As I returned to New Jersey after spending a subdued Christmas with my family, I thought about what had happened in that week of school before break – and what we faced in the weeks ahead. I had relied on the support of many during that week. I had relied so much on the Crisis Team members who thoughtfully crafted the school's response to the tragedy. I appreciated the school's administrators who stepped up when Joe, our "deputy" principal, became critically ill. I was grateful for our superintendent's wisdom and his support of my leadership.

But we had a precarious road ahead of us. Joe remained in the hospital, and it appeared that he might not return to work for a long time, if ever. My partners on the Crisis Team and I also knew that the school needed to re-focus on the mental health of our students. A year before the tragic car crash – before I came to work at the school – another SBHS student committed suicide in Manhattan by plunging 23 floors inside a Times Square hotel. We were deeply concerned about a potential suicide contagion effect that might particularly impact our most vulnerable students.

As the staff of the school returned to work after winter break, we started to tackle our priorities. We distributed Joe's responsibilities among four administrators, and they executed them well through the remainder of the school year. Knowing how efficiently Joe worked, they rose to that standard and made certain they worked together as a team.

We attended to mental health issues in the school by ensuring that key staff, like guidance counselors, social workers, and special education case managers, monitored vulnerable students closely for the rest of the year. The Crisis Team also reviewed and improved our response protocols for students struggling with their mental health, and we revisited how we trained our entire staff on these topics.

That first year, in leading key staff members and working together to respond to the serious developments, I learned many lessons that have stayed with me.

- **Respect each other's areas of expertise.** Administrators, counselors, and teachers are good at different things. Even our hall monitors, we found, had much to contribute as our "eyes and ears" among students. We needed to rely on one another and listen intently. Our crisis responses were better because we honored each other's knowledge and skills and listened to each other.
- **Make real-time adjustments.** As we dealt with the crises, it wasn't unusual for us to call impromptu meetings and adjust plans based on new information. We tried, however, to ensure that those adjustments were carefully considered, consensus decisions.
- **Communicate, communicate, communicate.** In times of crisis, it's nearly impossible to over-communicate. Even if there's not new, substantive information to share, people want to be reassured regularly that leaders are doing what they need to do.

We survived that terribly distressing December of my first year as a principal because key members of the staff pulled together. The professionalism and connectedness of many enabled us to move forward.

EMPATHY AS THE FOUNDATION

Among the team members who contributed most effectively to our crisis response in 2004 – and throughout my eight years as principal – were those who were able to connect best with students and colleagues. They exemplified empathy. They were able to truly understand the feelings and experiences of others. Empathetic leaders are able to forge deep connections and "walk in others' shoes." They are attuned to the needs of the people they serve, and they nurture empathy among their colleagues. They understand, as Rudyard Kipling wrote in the *Jungle Book*, that "the strength of the Pack is the Wolf, and the strength of the Wolf is the Pack."

One doesn't immediately think of football coaches when the topic of empathy comes up, but Doug Pederson exemplifies this as head coach of the 2018 Super Bowl Champion Philadelphia Eagles. Pederson is an unassuming leader who is more likely to express wisdom in plain language than flowery speeches. The Eagles had a particularly rocky path to the Super Bowl. During the regular season, in the wake of losing a number of key players to injury, including quarterback Carson Wentz, Pederson struck just the right tone of determination and optimism that the team needed to hear. The Eagles' journey to the championship demonstrated that the down-to-earth coach knew exactly what his players needed to hear at each step of the way.

Football coaches don't typically fit the popular image of the empathetic leader. That stereotype is characterized by group-hugging bosses who tell their team members how *wonderful* they are. Think of a caricature of Oprah or the exact opposite of Steve Jobs. Yes, empathetic leaders understand what team members are feeling, but that doesn't mean that they coddle. It means walking in their shoes, not indulging them. An effective empathetic leader uses her skills to assess where a team is at in light of the organization's vision, values, and goals – and then responds accordingly.

In staying well-attuned to the team, the deeply connected leader is particularly aware of three essential needs of whomever they may be working with. No matter what the endeavor, people working towards goals together need significance, order, and the opportunity to grow.

Something significant. Empathetic leaders are first attuned to a need we all experience: significance. We all want to be a part of something bigger than ourselves. We all want to feel that what we do is significant and meaningful. As Victor Frankl wrote in *Man's Search for Meaning*, "The more one forgets himself – by giving himself to a cause to serve or another person to love – the more human he is and the more he actualizes himself."

Toronto's Daveed Goldman and Nobu Adelman have smartly tapped into this desire. While singing in the shower (or in my case alone in my car to One Direction hits) can be enjoyable, it's a lot more fun to make beautiful music with friends, old and new. In 2011, Goldman and Adelman founded the weekly drop-in singing event called Choir! Choir! Choir! (C!C!C! for short). Participants, as they arrive for one of Goldman and Adelman's events, receive a copy of the lyrics for the song to be performed. Then the two leaders teach the arrangement to the assembled crowd, and they perform it while a video is made of the group's performance. C!C!C! events are held twice weekly at a bar in Toronto, and the pair also tours occasionally directing audiences throughout the world. Performing songs ranging from Louis Armstrong ("What a Wonderful World") to Green Day ("Basket Case") to the Muppets ("Rainbow Connection"), C!C!C! relies entirely on the talents of whoever shows up – and that's a big part of the magic.

In January 2018, Adelman and Goldman were joined by hundreds of New Yorkers at Manhattan's Public Theater. Their guest soloist in performing the David Bowie classic "Heroes" was David Byrne of the Talking Heads. After the experience, Byrne wrote in his blog,

> "There is a transcendent feeling in being subsumed and surrendering to a group. This applies to sports, military drills, dancing... and group singing. One becomes a part of something larger than oneself, and something in our makeup rewards us when that happens. We cling to our individuality, but we experience true ecstasy when we give it up."

Hundreds of South Brunswick High School students clearly demonstrate that they understand what David Byrne means when they show up for hours and hours of practice with the school's distinguished Marching Band. Led for many years by husband-and-wife music instructors Mark and Ginny Kraft, the band is consistently the best high school unit in the Northeast. Student musicians and flag corps members between June and December dedicate much of their "free" time to the communal joy of doing something truly excellent. Despite the band's demanding schedule, hundreds of students buy into the vision of working really hard to create something of real significance – a visually and musically beautiful performance.

Employees of New York restauranteur Danny Meyer are also attracted to be part of something significant: Meyer's network of eateries sets an international standard for hospitality. Meyer built an empire that began with New York's Union Square Café and now includes the high quality fast food service of Shake Shack. Through good hiring and training, Meyer built a strong culture of hospitality. His employees believe that they're doing something valuable and significant for customers by presenting them with a really positive experience – whether it's a great special occasion dinner or eating a great burger. Meyer's employees aren't just putting food in front of you; they're trying to make your day with great hospitality.

Meyer's approach not only shows his powerful empathy as a businessman but also demonstrates his commitment to empathy as a trait among his employees. Meyer explains, "The word thoughtful always exists when true hospitality is present, because it's somebody who is both thinking and feeling. That's what thoughtful means. It's thinking and feeling. You have to use your brain and your heart. If you're not using your heart, it's probably not genuine and therefore it's not authentic."

The right kind of order. Secondly, leaders must create the right kind of order in which team members can achieve their potential. Humans have a deep-seated need for order – it's why we wrote a Constitution in 1787 and it's why we continue to create by-laws and post company policies. But the order we create as leaders can't be capricious or arbitrary. Leaders have to understand how their colleagues are experiencing the sense of order they create. Is it too tight? Too loose? Is it fostering the values of the organization?

I always thought of my role as a school principal as being responsible for creating the most ideal environment so that teachers can best teach, and students best learn. The order that a leader creates must be developed and implemented fairly with alignment to values, vision and goals. The right kind of order creates the conditions in which people can achieve their potential.

As a first-year principal, for example, I noted almost from the first day of school, a long line of students queued outside the Attendance Office every morning as they checked in after being tardy for school. They were late *because they could be*. There were no real sanctions on their behavior. As a result, I led the administrative team in reassessing how we handled tardy students. When students actually starting getting consequences for chronic tardiness, a few parents complained at a School Board meeting. Our new approach was quite fair – the consequences started with a warning – and aligned with our values around the importance of responsibility and being in class. District leadership affirmed our approach at the Board meeting, and we moved forward. The changes significantly reduced the line of dozens each day to just a trickle. More students got to class on time so that they and their teachers could do their best work.

Opportunity to grow. The third fundamental need that empathetic leaders attend to among their employees is the desire to grow. None of us – writer, student, employee, or parent – want to feel like we're stagnating. All of us want to feel like we're making progress and getting a little bit better at what we're doing.

Giving the right kind of feedback can help team members make the kind of progress you and they hope for. Having been one of the lead architects for New Jersey's evaluation system for teachers, I have been on the giving and receiving ends of feedback for many years. Here are a few keys I've identified for feedback with an impact. Feedback should be

- **Specific and actionable.** Vague statements like "Needs to improve communication skills" don't help someone move forward. However, "Needs to contact clients proactively to discern their satisfaction with current services" might help an employee focus more on the real problem.
- **Encouraging.** In order to grow, we need to believe we can grow. Leaders who convey a belief in an employee's capacity to grow are more likely to see it. As we heard from teachers during my leadership of the state's Office of Evaluation, they were more likely to improve to grow when they received constructive feedback and heard their supervisor express confidence in their ability to grow. (Think: "Here's how you can get better" *and* "I know you can do it.") Research affirms this reality for employees in all kinds of roles. One of my favorite practices of a former boss, Superintendent Tom Westerhaus, was a handwritten note he called "A Drop for Your Bucket." On a specially made card shaped like a drop of water, Tom wrote notes addressing specific positive aspects of an employee's work. I still have a couple of notes that Tom sent me when I was an assistant principal.
- **Timely and honest.** I've often told people who work directly with me that they'll always know where they stand. I try to provide real-time, project-specific feedback. I never want employees to have to wait until a year-end review to find out how they're doing. That kind of wait is almost

inhumane. (One caution: If you're feeling angry or impatient about how an employee is handling something, then try to sleep on it before addressing it. I am *usually* pretty good about this.)

While empathetic leaders know their team members need order, significance, and opportunities for growth, they also know this isn't *everything* their employees need. Employees also need autonomy and compensation that reflects effort. But leaders who create the right conditions for employees to do their best work as described above will set their organizations on a path toward achieving their most important goals.

STAYING CONNECTED

Empathetic leaders know that communication is essential to building strong connections. I encourage leaders to think about four approaches to connecting with employees that bear great results: visibility, rapport-building, traditional modes of communication, and service.

Visibility, accessibility, and micro-impressions. When I was interviewing for the principal's position at SBHS, I was asked about how I would establish credibility as a relatively young administrator (37 at the time) with no principal's experience running one of the New Jersey's largest schools. I explained to the interview committee that I would build credibility through the thousands of small things that people notice, which I called "micro-impressions." These include qualities of basic good human interaction (calling people by name, looking them in the eye, and a firm handshake) to more job-specific impressions (preparing for a meeting by knowing the issues well or being able to articulate sound pedagogical practices, for example). Another reliable indicator of a principal's effectiveness is whether she picks up garbage when no one is watching.

I tried to be mindful as I interacted with staff and students that I was constantly being watched: How does Mr. Matheney talk to the custodial staff? Does he smile and say hello? Does his personal appearance express pride in his school and his job? Does he show up to meetings on time? Does he ensure that meetings are purposeful?

Sometimes I did things intentionally to create an impression among those who might be watching me. One example occurred regularly in the cafeteria. I think every high school struggles to get teens to throw out their garbage at the end of the lunch period. Though I didn't have time to do it as often as I'd liked, I tried to show students and staff in the cafeteria that I wasn't above helping out.   I'd push around a big garbage bucket on wheels and encourage students to drop in their refuse. This sent a message that I was committed to keeping the school clean. It also gave me a chance to greet students and be visible, which was especially important in a large high school. As a lunch session came to a close, I'd help push in chairs and toss remaining garbage into the buckets, despite the protestations of our great custodial staff. I wanted them to know that I valued their work and wanted to help out as much as I could.

At other times of the school day, when I was recovering from back-to-back-to-back meetings or an unpleasant phone call, I'd tell my secretary, "I have to get out of the office, pick up some garbage, and see some kids." During these quick tours of the school, my face would sometimes belie serious thoughts resulting from the meetings or calls. I readily admit that I may have failed to greet a staff member warmly and make eye contact from time to time when lost in my thoughts. Word occasionally got around to my secretary that "Mr. Matheney ignored me." The staff member worried that something bad was happening or that they were in trouble because I ignored them. Most of the time that wasn't the case at all – I was probably just processing an issue I had to work through. But I eventually learned, when I took those walks, to set aside my processing for a few minutes and just enjoy the walk. That led to many more friendly interactions with staff and students.

Sometimes, though, there were serious issues going on around school, and staff and students needed to see that I was serious about dealing with them. These were the times when I was most present around school. Students and staff needed to see that I was in charge, but still calm, cool, and collected. During one of the worst weeks I experienced as principal, a parent wrote in an email, "Thank you for being out there in the halls and not always at your desk (yes, word gets out)." I'm glad that her son and others had noticed. I appreciated her encouragement.

Clearly, the size of larger organizations like a Fortune 500 companies or army divisions make it much harder for a CEO or commanding officer to have the same kind of presence as a high school principal. Nevertheless, Steve Jobs strongly believed in the value of face-to-face interactions. He believed that creativity was well-served by spontaneous meetings, random discussions, and serendipity. Jobs had a significant hand in the design of both the Pixar and Apple corporate campuses, both of which foster the kinds of informal conversations that I enjoyed with teachers and other staff members as I walked through the school.

Building rapport. When I was an assistant principal (AP) dealing with all kinds of issues – from drug offenses to eggs flying over the third-floor balcony – I'd often come home and tell my partner at the time, "I made another boy cry today."

I didn't mean that I was intimidating or emotionally manipulative. I found, as an AP, that if you work to build a rapport with students by modeling restraint, calm, and kindness, they usually ended up feeling great remorse. Raising your voice never helped reduce recidivism in the assistant principal's office. I called my strategy "getting in under the radar." When teenagers' defenses are up, it's very hard to get them to listen. I deliberately worked to get students to remain open and engage in an honest conversation.

If I were dealing with a student after a fight, for example, I'd ask the student to give me a simple statement of the facts. They'd start giving me a rundown which was usually a rather distorted version of the truth.

I'd respond, "Now that's interesting, but tell me what's really going on."

And if, after hearing the student's response, I wasn't satisfied. I'd say again, quietly, gently: "Now that's interesting, but tell me what's really going on."

Eventually, we'd get down to the underlying issues. Then if I knew the student and his relationship to his parents, I'd go to my homerun swing:

"I know what you did wasn't really *you*. I know what you're capable of. Let's get your mom on the phone so you can tell her what happened."

At that point, it wasn't unusual for the crocodile tears to really flow, even among the toughest of students. Some of them begged me not to make that phone call.

The point of this approach was to make the issue about the behavior and the underlying issues, not about me as an authority figure or the student as a "bad kid." As soon as you make it clear by your demeanor and tone that you're focusing on actions, not labels, then a productive relationship can progress. And it often did.

The name game. Last fall, I visited a high school classroom where rapport clearly hadn't been built. More than a month into the school year I was touring the school with the principal when we stopped by a classroom at the beginning of the period. The teacher started the class by "reading the roll." Students answered "present" as they heard their name read. I felt like I had crossed over into a 1950s black-and-white movie.[1] Once that task was completed – which unnecessarily wasted instructional time – the teacher began to identify students to assist in going over the homework. As students raised their hands, the teacher just pointed and said, "Okay, you...and you...and you." At that point, I was deeply annoyed as it was apparent that the teacher didn't know the names of the students in her class. Inexcusable.

Fortunately, in the hundreds of classrooms I've visited, I found situations like that rare. Even in classrooms where the instruction was poor or mediocre, teachers typically could call students by name.

Sadly, though, college instructors get away with anonymous classrooms far too often. It may be understandable in a large lecture hall with 200 students, but not for smaller classes with a dozen or two students. It's true that it's easier in high school to learn names when teachers see students more frequently. But that's no excuse. When I started teaching at the University of

---

[1] A majority of high school teachers today just use a seating chart. The teacher takes a quick look at the classroom, and if students are not in their seats, they're marked absent. Pretty simple and quick.

Minnesota, with classes of 25-50 students meeting once or twice a week, I recognized the challenge of learning my students' names. A colleague suggested a simple trick: Bring a Polaroid camera to class, take photos of the students in groups of three or four, and then have them write their names under their image on the photos. And then, the critical last step: Practice! Sadly, my college students had low expectations, so when I nailed about 80-90% of the students' names at the next class, they were impressed. The only students whose names I struggled with were the ones who skipped a lot of classes, and I didn't feel that badly for them.

While it may seem like common sense, the first step toward establishing rapport is treating people as individuals. A surprising number of schools and principals make this error. Here are some of my pet peeves:

- School publications including newsletters and programs with misspelled names of students
- Awards programs and graduation ceremonies where students' names are mispronounced
- Teachers who frequently refer to and/or make comparison to a student's siblings
- Administrators who fail to ensure that new staff members and students are properly welcomed to the school community

Clearly, there are analogs to practices in other types of organizations as well. It all comes down to valuing the individual. At SBHS, with about nearly half of our families drawn from Asian countries, it was especially important to get the names right at graduation. Our student leaders who read the names at the ceremony practiced dutifully and made us proud every year.

While we all make mistakes – in print and otherwise – it's about the attitude toward striving to get it right. Organizations need to make every effort to get it right – and when they make honest errors, apologize profusely.

Traditional communication. How organizations communicate formally, even in an age of email and social media, still matters. I'm amazed when web sites have dead links and outdated information or when leaders fail to respond to email in a timely way. In all the organizations I've led – the high school, two state government offices, and the Philadelphia Academy of School leaders – we worked hard to maximize the usefulness of our web site, provide regular digital news updates, and ensure that staff responded in a timely way to email.

During critical incidents around the high school, like the time some science lab chemicals were spilled when being moved, we tried to be especially good about communication. After we took proper precautions around the chemicals and broken glass, I then sent a reassuring email to parents providing a few details with the clear message: "At no time was any student placed in harm's way." One parent responded to me immediately: "I want to commend you for ALWAYS keeping parents in the loop on anything that transpires in your school – good or bad." With nearly every student in the school carrying a cell phone, I always wanted parents to hear the story from me first whenever possible, not via text from their son or daughter.

Though he served in our highest office before digital communication became the norm, President George H.W. Bush serves as a great role model for effective communication. He is known for penning heartfelt letters to family members, political friends and foes, and leaders of other nations. Always a model of class, Bush left a handwritten note for his successor, Bill Clinton, in the Oval Office. The letter, which Clinton found on his Oval Office desk after his Inauguration, provided encouragement for the young Chief Executive:

> "There will be very tough times made even more difficult by criticism you may not think is fair. I'm not a very good one to give advice; but just don't let the critics discourage you or push you off course.
>
> "You will be <u>our</u> President when you read this note. I wish you well. I wish your family well.
>
> "Your success is now our country's success. I am rooting hard for you."

I have tried to follow Bush's example. I still send handwritten notes, though not as often as I'd like. I also treasure all the handwritten notes from my parents and grandparents that I've kept. Emails can certainly be touching and insightful, but the Luddite in me still believes that handwritten notes create a visceral connection between the writer and the reader that a digital message cannot.

Service and taking action. During the implementation of the new educator evaluation system in New Jersey which I led from 2012-2014, we believed that service to educators and districts communicated one of the most important messages of the initiative. We did not want to be aloof policymakers stuck in our offices in the state capital. Instead, I wanted our team to be as accessible and as helpful as we could be.

Effective policy implementation involves both skill and will, and we were determined to support both. We needed to have the technical know-how to help school districts strengthen their capacity to implement better teacher and principal evaluation systems. We also knew that we needed to win hearts and minds, and we couldn't do that sitting in a state office building. Our outreach efforts were led by three implementation managers, Bob Fisicaro, Anthony Fitzpatrick, and Paul Palek, all veteran educators. They were constantly on the road meeting with district leaders and talking to teachers. Other members of the team also participated in the outreach, and I spoke to audiences across the state as well. We accepted nearly every invitation offered. We participated in meeting with district administrators, school leadership teams, school board members, and associations of specialists (athletic trainers and speech-language-hearing specialists, for example). I particularly enjoyed the time I spent with the New Jersey Association of School Librarians, probably because librarians had been so important to me as a young reader.

Because expectations were so low for the Department of Education and other state offices, our team regularly exceeded expectations for accessibility and responsiveness. We returned phone calls, showed up for appointments, and followed up on our commitments. I was pleased when I heard from districts about how helpful we were, though I was saddened that they found the way we treated them to be atypical for a state government office.

Our team didn't just meet with receptive audiences. We didn't shy away from entering the proverbial lion's den – the New Jersey

Education Association, the state's powerful teachers' union, which wasn't on board with much of our policy agenda. My boss at the time, Peter Shulman, and I frequently met with the NJEA. Though they often disagreed with us, they had to admit that we were accessible, and we listened.

Even though our "products" were quite different, I know that my approach to the Office's belief in service was influenced by restauranteur Danny Meyer and others who stressed topnotch service. I talked with my team about how we could strengthen our credibility by the quality of service that we provided. I spoke of flawless execution. I knew, just as Danny Meyer preaches, that in serving others well, we also serve the interests of the organization.

SUSTAINING LEADERSHIP

Leaders not only need to foster connectedness in their organization, but they need to benefit from it as well. The demands on a leader, in a world with "24/7" communications and expectations, are endless. When a leader is trying to be accessible, communicate effectively, ensure the highest quality service, and meet the needs of his or her organization, the level of responsibility is exhausting.

Essential to surviving as a leader under such conditions are supportive relationships with important people in our lives. These connections are the roots of a leader's life – the deeper the roots, the more sustainable the leadership.

Two particular kinds of relationships help to sustain leaders during their hardest days: First, everyone with great responsibility needs to experience the loyalty and support of a cheerleader. Second, those leaders who make an enduring impact know the deep roots of unconditional love.

Today, my partner Ken is my greatest advocate. We've been together for six years, and he believes more in me than I believe in myself. He nurtures my dreams. Before I met Ken, a special colleague played that role. She still cheers me on today as a valued friend.

I first met Maryann Murphy when I became principal of SBHS. She was an assistant principal's secretary at the time, and I always appreciated her efficiency and friendliness, but I didn't know her well. I grew to appreciate her intelligence and skills when she accepted a promotion to work in the main office for my deputy, the school's Assistant Principal for Academic Leadership. When my secretary retired, I "stole" Maryann from him. Any CEO will tell you that his or her administrative assistant is a powerful role, and Maryann exercised her authority in that position with wisdom and intelligence. She solved a number of problems before they got to me, she calmed distressed parents, and she became the school's unofficial public relations director. Today, she still performs those roles for my successor.

Even more significant than her outstanding skills, Maryann's greatest gift to me was her unfailing support and loyalty. She always believed in me and my judgment. I always knew I had someone on my side. Her confidence in me helped me be a better leader. Yes, critical friends are important. But I believe we underestimate the value of people like Maryann who truly believe in us.

Cheerleaders are important people as we weather the ups and down of life we all experience. There are certain people, though, in everyone's lives who are foundational to our values and resilience. They are at the very roots of who we are as people. Reflecting on my life, I've grown to recognize that the foundation of my ability to connect with others in a deeply fulfilling way has surprising origins.

Margaret Sue was born into deep Southern poverty more than a century ago. Her mother gave birth in a glorified shack with dirt floors in Nelson Holler ("Hollow" for northerners) about 80 miles south of Nashville. Her father was a subsistence sharecropping farmer, who tended fields alongside former slaves in the late 1800s. He taught Margaret Sue never to judge people by the color of their skin, but only by the strength of their work ethic. It was a lesson she never forgot and always passed on.

Few opportunities existed for a young woman like Margaret Sue in pre-Depression rural Tennessee, but she made the most of the few she had. She dutifully completed her school lessons through eighth grade, but that was it. As a girl, she was expected to start helping out at home after grammar school.

Perhaps a few in the closest small town, Lawrenceburg, noticed that Margaret Sue was a bit sharper than most. A young man named Leo, who had earned his high school diploma and had higher aspirations, eventually courted her. Leo was interested in politics and had completed a year or two of college. Despite his moodiness and explosive temper, he was thought of as good husband material in Margaret Sue's limited world. Eventually they married, and Leo began a succession of jobs that provided a modest living for the young family. In the 1920s, for example, Leo was the teacher for a one-room schoolhouse, though Margaret Sue often claimed she was the one who did most of the work.

With his moods and his womanizing, Leo was a difficult husband. But Margaret Sue put up with him because he always had a job, and their growing family had food on their table, which was better than most as the Great Depression took root.

Despite the desperate economic times, Leo always seemed to have a sense of where the jobs were, which took the family in the early 1940s to Oak Ridge, Tennessee. Because of a hand withered by a fire in his childhood, he wasn't eligible to serve in World War II. But he still managed to get a job as a security guard. It was in Oak Ridge, where the young family, now with three children, enjoyed a brand-new government-built home surrounded by other families whose fathers and mothers had various roles building the atom bomb. (Leo, also known for his sense of humor, later liked to tell people that he was responsible for protecting the nation's atomic secrets.[2]) With a good job and a new home, one child later recalled, the family's time in Oak Ridge was one of their happiest.

After the war, the family moved again and again in pursuit of good wages. Each time, Margaret Sue, the glue of the family, would muster the kids and the family's belongings for the next destination. She made sure the children were clean (she was fastidious about her own appearance), got to school, and did their homework. Like so many women of the era, deprived of education and careers, she put her energies into the family. She was the nurturer and the children's defender when Leo got into one of his moods. Amid the transient life the children experienced, their mother was the rock. She was the leader of her family.

---

[2] He exaggerated obviously, but there was a kernel of truth to it. See, for example, newrepublic.com/article/120482/inside-oak-ridge-birthplace-atomic-bomb and *The Girls of Atomic City* by Denise Kiernan.

After the war, the family joined the migration of so many Southerners to northern industrial cities that held the promise of a stable, working-class living. Leo was hired as a technician – he was always good at math – at an oil refinery in Toledo, where some of Leo's family had already moved. Five hundred miles from home, Margaret Sue desperately missed her extended family, but immersed herself in being a homemaker and mother. The family was eventually able to buy a house in a blue-collar section of town with a sizable lot and a large apple tree. Despite more trials with Leo and the challenges of raising three kids mostly by herself, Margaret Sue became comfortable in her new life up north.

A world away. Seventy-six years after she was born in a Tennessee holler, Margaret Sue – or just Sue as she was called up north – walked unsteadily across the campus of one of the world's premier institutions of learning, Princeton University. Her daughter held her closely, while the family pointed out landmarks and mentioned some of the famous people who had walked that campus – Albert Einstein, an actor she loved, and Woodrow Wilson, the president when she was born. But Sue – my Grandma Sue – was just happy to be there because I was her grandson. In poor health with only a few years remaining with us, she insisted on making the trip. This little woman from rural Tennessee with an eighth-grade education was one of the most important influences in my life.

Through sheer acts of will, Grandma Sue worked hard to ensure that her children had better lives than her own, and she was successful. She was an affectionate grandmother who gave my brother and me the sense that we were the two most important people in the world. Years after her death in 1992, her unconditional love still resonates deeply with both of us. That's a powerful love. My brother and I were fortunate to have good parents who loved us, but we agree that there was no better example of *unconditional* love in our lives than Grandma Sue's. Her love forged the foundation for the many deep connections we have with our family and friends.

As I think about the deepest roots for my leadership, I return to the example of Grandma Sue who lived for her family and unconditionally loved us. I worked hard for good report cards, awards, and achievements all through school, and I knew Grandma Sue was proud of what I accomplished. But she didn't love me for all that. She loved me because I was her grandson. Nothing else mattered that much. I never needed to prove myself worthy of her love, and I knew that. It would *always* be there. Even today, Grandma Sue's unconditional love remains at the root of my leadership and my life. I know that so much of my ability to connect and love is a reflection of that little lady from Tennessee.

CHAPTER FOUR

COMMIT

To be honest, as principal at South Brunswick High School (SBHS), I would get a little jealous of physical education (PE) teachers on sunny spring mornings. As I took calls from irate parents or surveyed the dozens of emails in my inbox, I'd see them laughing with their students as they played soccer or Ultimate Frisbee on the freshly cut green fields of our campus.

It was one of those mornings one Friday in 2008 when a young, energetic PE teacher eagerly collected the appropriate gear for class and led her students outside to release some adolescent energy.

As the students headed out to the athletic fields, I had just completed my mid-morning walkthrough of the high school. I returned to the principal's office to take another look at my inbox, with my thoughts straying to the weekend. May was almost upon us – and that meant that an already busy school year was about to speed into its final six weeks.

As principal of a large school with more than 100 sports teams and activities, I was gearing up for the onslaught of tournament games, end-of-year banquets, and awards programs that contributed to a lot of 14-hour work days in May and June. After four years at the helm of this school, I knew that the last six weeks of school were the most exhausting months of the year. So on that Friday in late April, I looked forward to a quiet weekend to rest up for the final weeks of the school year – maybe plant a few flowers, maybe take a couple of naps with the cat.

As the class period drew to a close, the PE teacher, enthusiastic and friendly, rounded up the students on the athletic field and began to lead them across the parking lot full of staff and student vehicles toward the locker rooms. The teacher chatted amiably with a few students as they walked toward the school building when she picked up on a few snippets of a conversation from another group of students laughing nearby:

"... Banana boat ..."

"... Every morning by the park in our neighborhood ..."

"... Wonder why she gets a ride all the time ..."

Her instincts told her that what she heard didn't make sense. The "banana boat," which was parked nearby as the class headed into school, was a distinctive yellow pick-up truck driven by another PE teacher. It wouldn't make sense, she thought to herself, that her colleague would be parked in a neighborhood in the township every morning. He lived in another town that wasn't even that close by. And who would he be giving a ride to?

The teacher also knew that high school kids, particularly in a town referred to by its residents as "Mouth Brunswick," gossiped a lot, with much of the information lacking veracity. But there was something about what the teacher heard that morning that led her to think twice about what she heard. Something made her think, "Wait. There could be something more to this. This doesn't feel like the usual student chatter."

After her students changed out of their gym clothes and headed to their next class, the teacher shared what she heard with her supervisor. He listened to her account and agreed that the information raised some concerns. He didn't hesitate. "We've got to share this with Tim."

As the supervisor relayed the information to me minutes later, one part of my brain registered alarm, while another was skeptical: The teacher who drove the yellow pick-up had taught at the high school for several years and knew many alumni and parents in town. Maybe he was dropping off a package? Picking up equipment for the lacrosse team he coached in another school district? This is "Mouth Brunswick" after all, and students loved to speculate on teachers' personal lives. The information was vague, and I was very wary of launching an investigation about a teacher on the basis of the casual comments of students. Furthermore, it was already lunchtime. The school day would be over in a couple of hours, and I'd be heading home for the restful weekend my body craved. Wariness and convenience tried to convince me to ignore the students' comments – they were just kids joking around, right? – or at least go slow. A part of me said, "Just look into it on

Monday. This is what assistant principals are for. You can always have one of them do some interviews – maybe talk to the teacher."

But another voice reminded me where my values were as a principal. I thought about my first responsibility: to ensure that my students were safe. I deliberated for a moment then I told myself, "This is yours, Tim. Nobody else can handle this one. You've got to do your best work." Either a student's well-being or a teacher's reputation is at stake. *You have to get this one right.*

I jumped in. I started by looking up the names and addresses of the students involved in the conversation the teacher overheard. Yes, they lived near each other. I checked the street on MapQuest. Yes, there was a small park nearby. I made certain that the Banana Boat was, in fact, a teacher's vehicle. I looked up the address for the teacher and mapped the most obvious route he would take to school. There was no reason he'd come close to that neighborhood on his way to work. I knew also that our teachers at my school knew not to travel alone with students. It was a very strong norm. My gut told me there was something unsettling about all this.

By the time this issue arose, I had taken the lead on many serious investigations in my career – bomb threats, assaults, and more. Our administrative team would gather as much information as we could, then, if appropriate, share our findings with the police. In general, school authorities have a bit more flexibility in conducting investigations than the police do. We were always mindful that as soon as we believed a crime had been committed, we needed to share everything we learned with the police.

The assistant principals, the police, and I knew that this approach worked well. School administrators typically are able to get more information out of students than police officers. Students know us, and, in the case of SBHS, respected us. And kids instinctively start to clam up when a badge appears.

I wasn't reluctant, however, in other cases to get police involved immediately if I believed a student was in imminent harm. I knew that condition wasn't present in this case. Our students were safely in class. I knew, too, that I had a few hours until the school day ended to get a better idea of what was going on.

Convinced by the preliminary information I had, I decided there was a good reason to pursue an investigation. I gathered a couple of assistant principals, briefed them on what was reported, and identified the approach we would take:

- I would let the Superintendent know that we were looking into a potentially serious matter involving a teacher.
- The assistant principals would interview the students from the PE class.
- We would hold off on interviewing the owner of the yellow pick-up. I had to know if this was a case where he was falsely caught up in a malicious rumor mill or whether he was potentially in serious trouble before talking to him.

In about a half hour, the assistant principals generally confirmed what the students had said in PE class. Realizing the potential seriousness of the situation, the students had hedged just a bit. Maybe the vehicle with the yellow paint wasn't in their neighborhood *every* day, but, yes, they had seen it multiple times. One student reported that it seemed like the teacher was deliberately trying to hide, parking around a corner by the park.

In the meantime, I received a potential name for the girl, not yet 18, who'd gotten a ride on multiple mornings in the teacher's vehicle. I checked – yes, she lived near the talkative boys in the PE class.

With corroborated information about the teachers' presence in the neighborhood on multiple mornings before school, I decided it was time to talk to the girl whose name was shared with me.

As she made her way to my office, I reminded myself to take it slow. It takes time to get students to talk, but usually they will if you're patient. Besides, she had done nothing wrong. She was potentially, in a worst-case scenario, a victim.

She was clearly uncomfortable as she took a seat in my office, but not any more so than other students who got the call to see Mr. Matheney. I asked a female assistant principal to join us, and the three of us began to chat. Though uncomfortable, the student was poised and polite. I started our conversation as I generally did when questioning students with "How's everything going for you here at school?" In some cases, I got interesting information from that general question, but in her case, I didn't. She was having a good year, she told us, and she liked the high school. I had surmised that from looking at our student database: Her grades were good, she never got into trouble, and she was involved in school activities. She clearly was a good kid making her way toward college with no evident bumps along the way. But I sensed immediately that there was a reason for her reticence beyond the usual discomfort of being questioned in the principal's office.

After the initial chitchat, I asked her, "Have you seen a yellow pick-up truck parked in your neighborhood?

"No, I haven't."

"Are you sure? Maybe parked just around the corner from your house." I deliberately kept my voice calm and low.

"Yea, I'm pretty sure."

I persisted, but as gently as I could. I didn't want her to walk away from our exchange feeling that she was anything but a victim – if that was the case.

As my conversation continued, more information came out – a little at a time.

Yes, she had seen a yellow truck.

Yes, she had seen it multiple times.

Yes, she knew she had seen a teacher she recognized in the truck.

Yes, she had talked to that teacher in school before.

Eventually, I started to feel the progress of the interview begin to slow. More and more, I sensed the girl was protecting the teacher. From experience and training – and compassion – I decided to give her a brief break. I told her that I had to talk to my secretary. The assistant principal and I stepped out the office. I encouraged the administrator to keep chatting with the girl – ask her about her favorite class or plans for the weekend, that kind of stuff. We'd give her a chance to breathe, maybe relax a little bit without me in the room.

About ten minutes later, I reentered the office, told her how much we appreciated the information she had shared, and posed another question: "Have you ever gotten a ride to school from the teacher in the yellow pick-up?"

"Yes."

I tried to hide my surprise. The deeply serious nature of the situation was immediately clear to me.

As my questions continued, I paused a couple of times to remind her that she wasn't in trouble – that we weren't mad at her and that the teacher wouldn't be in trouble if he didn't do anything wrong.

At one point, I asked her if it was okay for us to keep talking – I didn't want her to feel like she was a hostage. "It's ok. I don't mind," she answered. The way she said it told me she wanted to tell us something important.

I pressed on.

Minutes later, she shared that she had had sexual contact with the teacher, and it had been, in her mind, consensual.

I immediately stopped the interview. I told her that I was sorry I hadn't become aware of this situation sooner. That we would support her in every way possible. But I was honest with her. I had to notify the police right away because I believed a crime had been committed, and I was obligated to inform them. They would want to talk to her.

A senior officer from the Police Department quickly arrived at school to take over the interviewing. The case was no longer in my hands, but I had gathered enough information for the Police and the Prosecutor's Office to pursue the case, which they did very quickly.

Along with the girl and her family, I spent that Friday night at the Police Department headquarters. I shared a formal, recorded account of the school investigation to the assistant prosecutor around 10 p.m. that night.

At some point in the early hours of the next morning – roughly 16 hours after the PE teacher overheard the joking comments about the Banana Boat – police officers arrested the teacher at his home. He was formally charged the next day with bail set at $200,000.

I later learned that the situation was far more serious than the student had told me. The prosecutor's officer later told the media that sexual contact had occurred between the student and teacher for more than five months.

The teacher's attorney told one reporter, "My client's a good guy." His client, the attorney said, "believed [the student] was ill and that's how the relationship started." He described his client's feelings for the girl as "love."

The teacher eventually pleaded guilty to child endangerment in a plea deal. He served jail time, gave up his teaching license, and never again stepped foot at my school after that Friday in April 2008.

WHAT WORKED

In the week that followed that Friday in April, as talk swirled around the community and the media began to publish their reports, I expected to be inundated by emails and voice mail. I was shocked, as the week progressed, to receive calls from only one or two parents. I let the parents voice their concerns. Then, without discussing the specific issue, I reassured them that the school took our students' safety very seriously. I also explained that I was very proud of our faculty, which was overwhelmingly filled with ethical professionals. The parents were satisfied, and the phone calls ended cordially.

But that was basically it. After the initial shock and disbelief, the community moved on within a few weeks. There were no passionate speeches before the School Board. No calls for community meetings. No accusations about the problem being larger than a single bad actor. I still marvel at how quickly the incident passed.

The quiet passing of such a significant incident resulted from values-driven leadership of many educators in the school district, led by Superintendent Gary McCartney. In the years preceding the incident, district leaders worked hard to affirm a student-centered approach. In the high school, our efforts at making our values of honesty, kindness, respect, responsibility, and service real for our students were beginning to make a difference. Parents saw that the values of the school and the district had solid roots, and they trusted the words and actions of administrators.

ROOTED IN PURPOSE

Deeply rooted values guided my decisions as a leader on that Friday in 2008. Unfortunately, there are far too many individuals and organizations with conflicted values who have failed to heed the kinds of signs that we encountered that day. We only need to look to the failed Catholic bishops, boarding school headmasters, and Penn State administrators and coaches who were more committed to preserving their institution's reputation than protecting children.

Those leaders failed to understand that maintaining the deep roots of an organization's values requires constant effort. The healthiest values-based organizations do several things very well:

- **Nurture values.** Leaders in these organizations reinforce the right values through storytelling and recognition. They highlight those people in the organization who exemplify the right values, and they share stories of how those individuals make an enduring impact.
- **Embrace transparency.** Leaders committed to a values-based approach embrace honesty. They are not afraid to stand before their stakeholders in an open dialogue.
- **Address toxicity.** Values-driven leaders know they must tend to their culture regularly and address negative behaviors as they arise.

Maintaining an organization's strong commitment to the right values clearly requires consistent attention. The high school's Leadership Team was acutely aware of this every spring as we considered personnel decisions.

In the first few years of my tenure, several departmental supervisors in the school took the path of least resistance. They posted a position, hired from the applicants, and at the end of that teacher's third year recommended him or her for tenure unless something had really gone wrong. They took the path of least resistance and made no effort to recruit. They accepted "good enough" because it was less work for them. Fundamentally, they didn't see hiring a teacher as the truly significant decision it is.

It wasn't always about taking the easier path. Some of those supervisors allowed other considerations to cloud their judgment as we met to discuss contract decisions for non-tenured teachers. They'd say things like

- "He has two children at home, and his wife's job's in jeopardy."
- "She teaches a subject that has a pretty thin pool of talent."
- "There are no red flags about him. He's doing a decent job."

When those considerations began to drive our conversation, I wasn't reluctant to steer us back on course. "We aren't an employment agency," I'd remind the group. "Yes, these are tough decisions, but our first responsibility is to our students. Students deserve the best possible teachers we can put in front of them."

The school district, fortunately, had a thorough, data-driven process with multiple evaluators for each non-tenured teacher. We made sure that one person's opinions were not sufficient to release – or retain – a teacher. As we made progress in the quality of our talent processes, we were much less likely to accept mediocrity. Students' lives, we knew, aren't changed by teachers who are "good enough."

LOSING YOUR WAY

Pilots, perhaps more than any other types of leaders, understand the cost of losing track of one's direction, even in a seemingly small way. All novice pilots learn the 1-in-60 rule. It's a rough estimate of the costs of miscalculating direction. For every degree a plane is off its proper path, the rule states, the pilot will find she's one mile off her destination. So, for example, if a plane is just a degree off course flying from Philadelphia to Chicago O'Hare (589 nautical miles), the pilot could end up looking for the airport as she flies over Wheaton or Schaumburg, Illinois, about ten miles from the correct destination. Oops. That small miscalculation could have potentially serious consequences.

Andy Hargreaves takes a similar perspective. Several years ago, I was fortunate to host the Boston College education professor during a session of the Philadelphia Academy of School Leaders. At one point during the day, Andy talked about the misperception that leadership is all about moving forward. "Leadership," Hargreaves pointed out, "is about both progress *and* direction." Leaders can lead. But *where* are they leading? Are they truly committed to the correct destination or will their chosen direction require them to look for a landing strip over their metaphorical Schaumburg?

Early in my administrative career, I saw evidence of school staff members, in a sense, losing their way. They put their comfort ahead of serving students. When I served as dean of ninth-graders at a school in Minnesota, an upset parent was directed to my office. She had just tried to enroll her son at the school. The mother told me that the family had to move unexpectedly, and the guidance counselor who was assigned to enroll the student told the mother to come back in two days. The staff member said her calendar was full. When I heard the mother's account, I was bothered by the lack of urgency. The student would likely miss two full days of instruction if the counselor's decision prevailed. I wondered if the mother had been dismissed by the counselor because of the family's circumstances. Perhaps the counselor thought that if the boy's family had to move "unexpectedly" – evicted? – then he was the kind of kid for whom another day or two out of school wouldn't matter.

I wasn't comfortable with the situation, and, even though I was just a few weeks into my tenure with the school, I headed over to the guidance office, leaving the mother and son behind in my office. I explained the situation to the guidance director and expressed my hope that the student would be enrolled more quickly. He told me that there were protocols for enrolling new students, and the counselors were a busy group. My blood began to boil, and I thought about raising the issue with the principal, who I knew to be a student-centered leader. But I kept calm and simply explained that it was a bad idea that a student – for whom we were now responsible – was going to sit at home for another two days. The guidance director finally relented and moved up the student's enrollment to the following day. I really wanted to hear something like, "Sure, bring the student over. I'll take care of it myself." But it was better than before, and the parent was satisfied. Later that day, the counselor left a voice mail for me saying she was very unhappy that I challenged her and her department's procedures. Once I listened to the message, I happily hit "delete."

A system that was off-course. The origins of collective-bargaining and union due process protections make a lot of sense. Any student of the Progressive Era knows that those reforms were necessary in light of rampant abuses in the workplace in the era of industrialization.

But by the time I became a principal in New Jersey, the teacher tenure system was out of balance. The case of one faculty member, whom I'll call "Tracy," drove the issue home for me. Tracy had struggled for years, despite encouragement and offers of assistance. Many parents who'd had a child in the teacher's classes in previous years refused to allow their younger children to have the instructor. At the beginning of each school year, we noted, out of the 80-100 students assigned to Tracy, as many as a quarter of them requested transfers.

Finally, one year, we discovered that Tracy was hoarding hundreds and hundreds of ungraded assignments. Students had completed the work, hadn't received feedback, and didn't know their grades on the assignments. The teacher taught critical classes, and I was deeply concerned students weren't getting the college preparation they needed. Despite clear evidence of poor performance, we were advised by the district's lawyer that it still wasn't possible to get rid of the teacher until we gathered more documentation. Tenure laws and due process requirements ensured that students in the classroom were stuck with, at best, mediocrity and, at worst, pedagogical malpractice. The legal framework of tenure protection for teachers in New Jersey at that time clearly protected the interests of teachers like Tracy over the interests of students.

After more time passed, and Tracy added more fuel to our concerns, we handed over a pile of documents about a foot tall to the lawyer secured by the district to handle the case. Only with that kind of leverage – which took hundreds of administrative hours to build – was the lawyer convinced we could get rid of the teacher. Ultimately, through persistence and the strong case, Tracy finally left the school after several years of well-documented incompetence.

After we heard of the teacher's plans to leave, the departmental supervisor and I sat relieved in my office. We talked about what we could have done with all the hours that had gone into the case. We could've spent our time helping other teachers get even better, strengthening the culture of the school, ensuring a great education for all students – but all those hours went into the case of only one teacher.

In 2012, the TEACH NJ Act was signed into law by Governor Chris Christie. The law, which created a more streamlined legal framework for exiting incompetent teachers, was a bipartisan effort to right the ship. Even the New Jersey Education Association supported the legislation, though they later showed some significant "buyer's remorse." To implement the law, the state had to create a new evaluation system for public school educators. Ready for a new challenge after eight years of leading the high school, I joined the Department of Education to lead the evaluation initiative. In that role, I was committed to creating a better balance between the interests of students and the interests of teachers.

Schools and school districts, like other organizations, lose their way. They place the interests and convenience of employees ahead of the clients they serve – students. Even for-profit companies do this. A small retail store just a few blocks from my home has a loyal clientele. The store has a unique inventory that attracts customers from the well-heeled neighborhoods of the city. But it's the kind of store that faces stiff competition from Amazon and large chains that sell similar products. Late last fall, the manager of the store told his staff that the store would be adding an hour to its scheduled hours for the holiday season. He then asked whether the hour should be added to the beginning or end of the current schedule. The employees agreed that adding an hour made sense and that the store should open *an hour earlier*, which clearly reflected a commitment to their own convenience, not their customers'. The staff of the store didn't care when shoppers might actually be likely to shop at the store – which probably wasn't at the start of the work day. This seemingly small decision – remember the 1-in-60 rule – reflected how the organization was veering off course. The store's leadership and its employees had forgotten that the purpose of the store was to serve its customers, not the convenience of its employees or managers.

Yes, the interests of employees do matter. A cold, heartless organization will eventually pay the price as talent flees for a better workplace. But the priorities have to be aligned. The interests of clients – whether they're students or retail customers – must be placed ahead of employees (and that includes management). If this doesn't happen, students will not receive the education they deserve, and the local retail store will cease to exist.

COMMITMENTS AND PLEDGES

From their earliest days, fraternities have emphasized character and values. Initiation rites almost always involve memorization of the fraternity's principles or doctrines. Sigma Alpha Mu, a fraternity founded in 1909, has a creed typical of many college Greek organizations:

> "To foster and maintain among its sons a spirit of fraternity, a spirit of mutual moral aid and support; to instill and maintain in the hearts of its sons love for and loyalty to Alma Mater and its ideals; to inculcate among its sons such ideals as will result in actions worthy of the highest precepts of true manhood, democracy, and humanity."

Similarly, Beta Theta Pi, founded in Oxford, Ohio in 1839, seeks to "Develop men of principle for a principled life." Among the fraternity's core values are "mutual respect," "responsible conduct," and "integrity."

My father pledged Sigma Chi at Bowling Green State University in the late 1950s. Years later he could still recite most of the fraternity's creed that called for "fairness, decency and good manners." He loved his college experience with Sigma Chi, remaining an active alumnus throughout his life. My father spoke fondly of the camaraderie, and my mom took great pride in being pinned a "sweetheart of Sigma Chi."

Greek life obviously has its benefits – friends for life, community service, opportunities to strengthen leadership and social skills. Fraternities raise more than $20 million every year for various charities. Sigma Chi alone has raised millions of dollars for the Huntsman Cancer Institute in Salt Lake City.

While many fraternities are clearly committed to service, leadership, and character, others veer wildly from their principles, placing their pledges and members at significant risk. These chapters lose sight of the real meaning of brotherhood.

Brett Griffin graduated from SBHS in 2008. He was a solid, 'lege-bound student, and a member of the wrestling team. I 'nber him as a polite kid who never got into any trouble. In 'l after he graduated, he headed to the University of Brett explored Greek life and decided to pledge Sigma 'he fraternity whose creed pledges "mutual moral aid By the end of a pledge party four months after his 'ation, he was dead.

According to media reports, Brett drank a 750-milliter bottle of Southern Comfort following an unwritten fraternity rule that a pledge is to consume a full bottle of alcohol with his pledge brother.   Toxicology reports subsequently found Brett's blood alcohol content to be .341. The legal limit to drive is .08.

Brett's death is recorded as the nation's 181st hazing-related death on a sad chronology maintained by Franklin College journalism professor Hank Nuwer. [3]

When I visited the funeral home after Brett's death, I saw the enormous pain in his grieving parents. I saw the photos from his childhood, from good times with his high school friends and family. His life was cut short because of a catastrophic failure of leadership and the fraternity's commitment to its enacted, not espoused values. The fraternity had placed its commitment to life-endangering binge drinking over the safety of its pledges.

Sigma Alpha Mu was subsequently banned from the University of Delaware. Brett's family eventually settled out of court with the fraternity and several of its members. However, they chose to pursue a wrongful death civil case against the fraternity's president and pledge master. In 2013, the former fraternity officers were found not responsible for Griffin's death. After the case, the pledge master told the *Wilmington News Journal* that the fraternity did "some dumb stuff but nothing ever to hurt anybody," adding, "I don't know what I could have done differently."

In 2014, a second SBHS graduate from my tenure at the school died from alcohol poisoning. Caitlyn Kovacs passed away after attending a party at the Delta Kappa Epsilon fraternity at Rutgers University in New Brunswick, New Jersey. The incident was not related to hazing. Caitlyn loved animals and was an aspiring veterinarian.

Tim Piazza was a well-liked student-athlete who attended high school about 25 miles from South Brunswick. He died in February 2017 after a particularly gruesome incident at Beta Theta Pi at Penn State University that was documented in the national media and a lengthy *Atlantic* article. Tim arrived at a pledge party shortly after 9 p.m. and a little more than an hour and a half later he appeared on security camera video to be in a drunken stupor. Shortly thereafter the young man fell down a flight of stairs, causing serious intern

---

[3] www.hanknuwer.com/hazing-deaths/

injuries. Despite his obvious physical distress and concerns voiced by several members, no one in the fraternity that promised to develop "men of principle for a principled life" called 9-1-1 until the next morning, 12 hours after his fall, when he was barely alive. Tim was the 219th hazing-related death on Nuwer's list. Four deaths, including Tim Piazza's, were added to the list in 2017. Thirty-seven college students died from hazing-related incidents between Brett's and Tim's deaths.

Nuwer's list is a sad testament to a fundamental breakdown of leadership and organizational values. These incidents point to the hypocritical gulf between the espoused and enacted values of some fraternities. Some of the deaths also point to a broader problem of college leadership, where alarming signals from the Greek system are ignored. Universities have the ability to place limits on the role of Greek organizations in college life and inhibit the irresponsible behavior of the worst fraternities. National offices of Greek organizations can assume more responsibility for training and accountability. Local Greek leaders must commit, above all else, to ensuring the safety of their members and pledges. Inevitably, when leadership fails, another name is added to Hank Nuwer's tragic list.

In an ironic quotation attributed to the late Penn State coach, Joe Paterno compared those "who cannot be detoured from their convictions" to those "who do not have the courage to have any convictions." There are abundant examples of organizations where there's talk about values, but their direction is clearly off course with sometimes catastrophic consequences. Fraternities like the ones in Brett Griffin's and Tim Piazza's deaths are two organizations that had the wrong set of priorities, resulting in terrible losses. We can also look to presidential administrations that care little about ethics and the Penn State football program that tolerated Jerry Sandusky's abuse of children for years. Values-based leaders and organizations that truly "cannot be detoured from their convictions" know that a genuine commitment to the right values requires constant vigilance and hard work to make those values meaningful.

STRENGTHENING VALUES-BASED ORGANIZATIONS

There's no fool-proof way for leaders to avoid becoming another case study of organizations that are seriously off-course. There are, however smart practices of those organizations who try to get it right. They include
- Developing and using a common language of values.
- Providing opportunities for enacting values.
- Ensuring alignment of values and practices.
- Conducting orientation and re-orientation to reinforce values.

A common language. Leaders will never be able to ensure perfect behavior within an organization. Humans are humans, after all. To get the best out of people, the consistent expression of values is essential. Common language about values provides a moral framework for people in an organization. An articulated set of values can also serve to constrain some of our most human instincts.

At SBHS, we lived by five core values: Honesty, kindness, respect, responsibility, and service. Thanks to teacher Martin Barbour, we even had a shorthand version: Strive for Five. I knew we had made strides in making the language part of our culture when our graduation speakers began to include references – often serious, sometimes funny, always respectful – to the motto and values.

We also made clear what language was not permitted. "Retarded," and other words that were used solely as put-downs were not tolerated in our hallways and classrooms. It wasn't about political correctness. We knew teenagers can be pretty abusive with language, and we sought to create a school that felt safe for all kinds of students.

These lessons required constant reinforcement. I remember one day I was walking the halls between classes. Because I'm short, I could easily blend in among students in a crowded hallway going from class to class. You'd be amazed at the things I heard. On this particular day, I heard a girl a few yards away tell a boy, "You're so gay."

By her tone I could tell she meant, "You're being ridiculous."

I stopped in my tracks with students piling up behind me and said loudly in my best principal voice, "Excuse me?"

She finally noticed it was me – her openly gay principal.

Turning red with embarrassment, "Oh, I'm sorry, Mr. Matheney," she said, "I didn't mean it. Really."

I had made my point.

"Just get to class. You know that's not how we operate around here. Don't do it again."

Getting teenagers to stop using "gay" when they mean "bad" or "distasteful" isn't easy. But it's a worthwhile effort. Addressing its use in that context sent all students within earshot an important message about the kind of school we wanted to create.

Enacting values. I've always believed that language and behaviors interact and shape each other. People who are led to do good things are more likely to express themselves in a positive way. Students or employees who hear and use positive, affirming language are more likely to act in positive ways. From my own days as a student to my years as a principal, I was amazed by teachers who were demeaning or caustic with students, but then expected students to participate in class or behave positively. Similarly, managers who are critical without being constructive can expect team members to be defensive and resistant. I learned this important leadership lesson early on as a kid at Sunday school: "What you sow," we learned from Paul's letter to the Galatians, "you will reap."

I've also found that the more people use positive language and engage in positive actions, the deeper their commitment will be to the values that the language and actions represent. Possessing the right set of values is like exercising a muscle. The more a child practices honesty – even in difficult circumstances – the more he'll find that in the long run, honesty works. The more a teenager practices responsibility, the more capable of being responsible she becomes.

Schools often tell children to be good and "do good", but they don't provide them enough opportunities to practice it. Leaders have to ensure that their colleagues and students have a chance to show how good they can be. One of my favorite initiatives to accomplish this at the high school was the Viking Closet, created by in-school suspension monitor Jennifer Webb to meet some unmet needs of the community. Jen knew that many students were outgrowing or no longer needed gently used clothing. She also knew we had families who desperately needed clothes, particularly for their growing teens. So, with the help of a dedicated group of students and staff, she created a clothing exchange inside the school. Jen's signature initiative is the "Sisterhood of the Traveling Prom Dress," which helps make prom more affordable by providing for the passing on of gently-used formal dresses. Almost ten years from its creation, grateful families in need still stop by the Viking Closet to pick out needed items from its constantly refreshed inventory. The Viking Closet enables students to be good and to "do good."

Alignment. The most admirable organizations carefully align what they say and what they do with the right set of values. They don't undermine the values listed in their mission statements with unethical or irresponsible actions that belie an entirely different belief system. They seek to practice consistency in beliefs, words, and actions. When people in the organization make bad decisions, the errors are addressed, and the organization gets back to work. Perfection isn't the goal; living a coherent organizational life is.

Howard Schultz, the man most responsible for making Starbucks ubiquitous, has a well-deserved reputation for aligning the company's values and practices. Among American retailers, Starbucks is known for its best-in-class approach to compensation. Starbucks was one of the first retail chains to offer full health-care benefits to store employees, even part-time workers. They have also provided access to a tuition-free four-year degree program through a partnership with Arizona State University.

One 2017 study by the employee services firm Aon found that the benefits provided Starbucks employees working 20 hours or more are three times more valuable than those provided any other retailer.

Schultz explains that Starbucks' actions aren't a result of happenstance. Rather, they follow an explicit philosophy. In his book Pour Your Heart Into It, Schultz writes, "Because not everyone can take charge of his or her destiny, those who do rise to positions of authority have a responsibility to those whose daily work keeps the enterprise running, not only to steer the correct course, but to make sure that no one is left behind."

Though far from perfect, we tried to achieve a strong alignment of beliefs, words, and actions at SBHS. We sought to integrate our focus on character with academics, athletics and activities. For example,

- We created a character-oriented comment bank in our online student academic database. Teachers, then, could include a positive comment about a student aligned to our core values.
- At pep rallies, which at most high schools are only about sports, we created a VIP section (with bean bag seating!) for students who had distinctive accomplishments in academics, music, and extracurricular activities.
- Each season, the Athletic Department presents the "Strive for Five" award to a male and female student-athlete who best represents the school's five core values.
- The honor roll includes a special category, "Principal's Distinction," that allows faculty members to nominate a student who has particularly lived out the school's values or demonstrated considerable academic growth.

Orientation and re-orientation. In the novel *The Art of Fielding,* author Chad Herbach writes, "A soul isn't something a person is born with but something that must be built by effort and error, study and love."

Organizations, in a sense, have souls, too, and leaders must deliberately attend to them. Harmony among a leader's or organization's beliefs, words and actions can't be taken for granted. The people of an organization need to participate in deliberate orientation and re-orientation for those messages to retain their important meaning.

Unfortunately, orientation for new employees in most organizations consists of signing tax forms, reviewing key company policies, and, if you're lucky, doing some kind of ice breaker to get to know your new colleagues. Inevitably, these days are typically spent in windowless rooms where the hours drag by slowly.

Orientation in the South Brunswick School District, in contrast, was a team effort. Joanne Kerekes, an outstanding assistant superintendent for many years, set the tone from the start for new teachers for the district's newest teachers as the first day of school approached. Joanne and the principals who assisted her shared the district's values and philosophies while modeling good pedagogy. After districtwide orientation, new teachers would spend time in their respective schools. In the high school, I had a special session with the group where I shared my homage to a David Letterman Top Ten List – except that my list articulated important aspects of our culture as a school. Here are four:

- **Ask for help.** There's nothing wrong with asking for help. It doesn't signify weakness. Successful teachers seek the advice of their peers and supervisors.
- **It's not all about you.** Don't take what kids say too personally. When they say things in anger or frustration toward you, it's nearly always *not* about you. When students act out, hold them accountable and get them the help they need from an assistant principal or counselor.
- **Be friendly, not a friend.** You always need to know where the line with your students is. Be wary of social media. Friendly, professional relationships are great, but keep it to that.
- **Go the distance.** Do whatever it takes to ensure that your students learn. Above all else, that's your job.

With students, we also intentionally conducted orientation and re-orientation to our school's core values. Two events in particular helped us achieve this. First, we introduced 9th graders to our values at our annual Convocation. This somewhat formal ceremony, which took place every September, was created several years before I became principal. But in my third year, we substantially tweaked the program and aligned it with our core values. We began to identify members of our staff who represented our values and asked them to speak for a few minutes about the value. We also presented awards to members of the school community who exemplified our values.

Later each school year, our activities coordinator and character education committee organized an annual presentation. We typically hosted a guest speaker: Kyle Maynard, author of *No Excuses: The True Story of a Congenital Amputee Who Became a Champion in Wrestling and in Life*, and Bobby Petrocelli, who wrote *Ten Seconds Will Change Your Life Forever*, were two favorites. We also hosted four incarcerated young people whose moving stories had a significant impact on our students.

We made certain these programs weren't just "one and done" events as so often happens in schools. We followed up with activities tied to the presentation's theme, provided suggested lesson plan tie-ins for teachers, and challenged the school community to achieve a goal. For example, after the event with Maynard, I challenged each student and staff member to perform two hours of community service in the following three weeks. (We didn't achieve the ambitious goal, but students and staff members admirably performed more than 1,500 hours of service in that short period of time.)

SHOW YOUR COMMITMENT

On a September day in 1981, my mother drove me to school in our poop-brown Chevy Chevette. It was my freshman year at the St. John's Jesuit High School in Toledo. With the support of my parents, I had decided to move from our local semi-rural school district to the all-boys Catholic school with a great academic reputation about 20 miles away. There were no direct school bus routes, so my mother often drove me to school until I earned my driver's license.

On that September morning about halfway through the trip, my mother turned down the radio morning show we always listened to and asked, "Are you okay? You're kind of quiet this morning."

I thought I was always quiet on that drive. I was usually half-asleep.

"I'm fine. Just tired," I said. In reality, I was a bit nervous. Shortly after my mom dropped me off at school, I was going to make a speech on the school's closed-circuit TV station. I was a candidate for class president. Though I had already done some public speaking before that, I was still anxious. Making a speech on TV and to the school itself was new to me. I arrived as a freshman there not knowing a soul. Though I'd made a few friends in my classes, I still felt like an outsider.

As we approached the final stretch of highway on the route to school, I felt my stomach churn.

"I know you're probably nervous about that speech," my mom said. "You're going to do fine. You're a great speaker. I know you'll win."

I closed my eyes and took a deep breath. "Thanks. I'm okay. But I'm not sure I'll win. Nobody knows me."

"They'll know you soon enough. Just relax. We're almost there."

We soon exited the highway and took the final turn into the school's parking lot. I felt jittery and a little nauseous about the speech.

My mother pulled up alongside the curb near the main entrance where other parents were dropping off their sons. I got out of the passenger seat and grabbed my backpack as my stomach did somersaults.

"You look pale. Are you sure you're okay?"

"No, not really."

Then I gagged and threw up that morning's bowl of Cheerios on the curb next to the Chevette.

I stood there a bit shocked. I looked at my dress shirt and tie. Nope, no vomit. My mom handed me a tissue to wipe my face.

"Do you want me to call you in sick?" She looked concerned.

I stood there for a second. "No, I'm fine," I said stoically.

"I'll see you after school. Love you," I said as I closed the car door. I headed toward the school entrance. Forty-five minutes later, still a bit nauseous, I read my speech.

Later that day, I lost the election to a classmate who wouldn't even finish out the year at the school. It was an ignominious beginning to my brief political career. But I was proud of myself that day. Despite my obvious trepidations – and, yes, the vomit – I was committed. *I showed up.*

I may not have been conscious of it at the time, but even as a 14-year-old I had internalized some important lessons about leadership. Good leaders are deeply committed to their goals. They know that being committed isn't about words, it's about actions. It's about showing up.

Even though he's a lightning rod for NFL fans outside of New England, Patriots quarterback Tom Brady consistently *shows up*. A three-time NFL and four-time Super Bowl MVP, Brady has already proven himself time and time again. There's clearly a reason for his success. As one observer noted, early one June morning in 2016, three months before the first game of the season, Brady arrived early for his team's veterans' mini-camp and took his seat in the front row of the meeting room. He was committed and prepared, a role model for the entire team despite his accolades. The following January, Brady and the Patriots won the greatest comeback victory in the history of the Super Bowl.

In stark contrast is a New Jersey school administrator I know. As a principal he was known for disappearing out the back door of his office. He'd head out to a local Dunkin' Donuts, sometimes taking an assistant principal with him. When he missed appointments for no good reason or wasn't present when a parent showed up in the office, his poor secretary had to make up excuses for him. His absence said volumes about how much he valued the hard work of school leadership.

In contrast to that principal, Admiral Paul Zukunft, Commandant of the U.S. Coast Guard, knows about keeping commitments. In 2017, when the White House proposed banning transgender troops from all branches of the military, Admiral Zukunft stood firm. He expressed support for the transgender members of the Coast Guard and made sure they received calls of support from the Commandant's office. Despite the real possibility such a stance could harm his career he vowed his support of the 13 known transgender members of the Guard. Zukunft made his support clear in public comments that August. "That is the commitment to our people right now," the Commandant said. Though small in number, "all of [the transgender troops] are doing meaningful Coast Guard work today."

When I was a high school dean, a mother of a student taught me one of my favorite lessons about commitment and showing up. I gave her a call one day to follow up on a minor discipline issue involving her daughter. Her daughter wasn't a "frequent flyer" in my office, so I wasn't overly concerned. But it was good practice to call home after meeting with a student.

When the mother answered the phone, I could tell that she was taken aback. I could tell that she hadn't received many calls like that one. She listened intently, asked a few questions, and said,

"Thank you so much for calling. I always support the school. You do what you need to do."

"Thank you, Mrs. Brown. But I'm confident this issue is over and done with."

"I certainly hope so. When my daughter gets home she will *certainly* hear about this conversation. All of my children they are forbidden to embarrass the family. If my daughter is a problem for you again, she will know that I'm going to return the favor."

"I promise you, sir," she continued, "that I will show up at school in pink fluffy slippers, my hair in curlers, and my front teeth blacked out, and demand to see you and all of her teachers. Let's see what my daughter thinks about embarrassing us then."

I could tell by her tone she was quite serious – and quite committed. If her daughter's behavior was ever in question again, I have no doubt that she was prepared to *show up*.

Not surprisingly, she never needed to. I never saw her daughter in my office again.

HE SHOWED UP

"To be a man is, precisely, to be responsible. It is to feel shame at the sight of what seems to be unmerited misery. It is to take pride in a victory won by one's comrades. It is to feel, when setting one's stone, that one is contributing to the building of the world."
— Antoine de Saint-Exupéry, *Wind, Sand and Stars*

Shortly after 9 a.m., on a beautiful September morning in suburban Minneapolis, Craig Olson, Dan Edwards, and I, the administrators at Prior Lake Senior High School, met urgently to discuss how to handle the news that was breaking that morning. Do we have students with parents in New York right now? Any staff with family connections in Manhattan? I thought of a couple of my college roommates who were probably at work in Manhattan. It was my sixth school day on the job as an assistant principal.

Twelve hundred miles away in Manhattan, Judy Wein waited in the 78th floor elevator lobby of the south tower of the World Trade Center. Seventeen minutes before, a plane had struck the neighboring North Tower. Wein considered returning to her office to retrieve her pocketbook, she told the *New York Times*, but her boss, Howard Kastenbaum, told her not to – that he'd give her the money to get home.

As Wein, some of her coworkers, and many others waited in the elevator lobby at 9:03 a.m. on September 11, 2001, United Airlines Flight 175 crashed diagonally into the 77th through 85th floors of the South Tower. When she awoke from the crushing blast, Wein surveyed her injuries, which were serious. But at least she could walk.

"I got up and walked to the people in my group, walking over bodies. They were all over," Wein. "I sat down, and Howard, my boss, was flat on his back and motionless, and I believe he was not alive. I [had known] him for 23 years."

Ling Young, an employee with the New York State Department of Taxation, was badly burned by the impact of the plane, but had survived in the same elevator lobby. As she and a few others near her gathered their wits, a mysterious man appeared, with a red handkerchief covering his mouth and nose.

"All [of] a sudden we saw a young man come out of nowhere. You heard this man's voice say, 'I found the stairs. Follow me. Only help the ones that you can help,'" she recounted. "It was the way he said it. We just got up [and followed]."

As Young's group made their way down the stairs, she noticed that the man was carrying a young woman on his back. Once they reached clearer air, she recalled, he put her down and "decided to go back up."

Minutes later, Wein and several more people in the 78th floor elevator were starting to move, too. Wein found four others who could walk, including one who was able to pry open an elevator door and climb out of a burning car. As they gathered their wits, the man with the red handkerchief found them. He was searching for a fire extinguisher. The man, the *New York Times* reported from Wein's recollection, once again "pointed to the stairs and made an announcement that saved lives: Anyone who can walk, get up and walk now. Anyone who can perhaps help others, find someone who needs help and then head down." At his urging, this second group of survivors started their precarious trek downward.

Welles Remy Crowther was a 24-year-old equities trader with Sandler O'Neill and Partners on the 104th floor of the South Tower when it was struck on 9/11. A 1999 Boston College graduate, he had been a member of the college's lacrosse team, where he played with a ubiquitous bandanna under his helmet. Through high school and college, he had been an honors student, and, at 16, he joined as a junior member of his local fire company in Upper Nyack, New York.

Nine minutes after the first plane struck the North Tower Welles called his mother Allison and left a voice mail. "I want you to know that I'm okay," he said. That was the last his parents would hear from him. At 9:59 a.m., 47 minutes after Welles' phone call to his mother, the South Tower collapsed. His father, Jeff, incredulously watched it fall on television.

Six months after 9/11, Welles' body was uncovered in a South Tower pit near members of the Fire Department of New York. The specific circumstances of Welles' death, however, remained a mystery – at least until May 2002 when his mother was reading a *New York Times* article that described the harrowing experiences of people in the towers on 9/11. When she got to survivor Judy Wein's account, she stopped reading. "The minute I saw the reference to the red kerchief" – the bandanna that Welles carried for years – "I went 'Oh my God, Welles. I found you.'" She quickly reached out to Judy Wein and Ling Young and shared photos of her son with them. They both confirmed the identity of the confident young man in the red bandanna. "That was him. There was no question in my mind," Young said.

Eyewitnesses on 9/11 believe Welles Crowther may have saved as many as 12 people that day, but probably would have been uncomfortable with the attention given his heroic story. "Welles was, more than anything, proud of other people, and he really took other people's accomplishments with greater pride than he did his own accomplishments," his sister Honor Crowther Fagan explains.

Welles was posthumously named an honorary firefighter by the FDNY, and his heroic acts were described by President Obama at the 2014 dedication of the National September 11 Memorial and Museum.

On 9/11, Welles Crowther was fully committed. His values, his words, and his actions became one. He showed up.

CHAPTER FIVE

PERSEVERE

2001: Minneapolis. It was a bitter January morning when I parked my car and made my way through the labyrinth of the University of Minnesota's underground trails – dubbed the "Gopher Way" – to avoid the brutal cold. I arrived in my spacious office in Wulling Hall, a quaint academic building in a quiet corner of the Minneapolis campus, and tossed my coat on my desk. As I thought through some of the words I'd say in just a few minutes, I scanned the hundreds of books I had carefully placed on bookshelves when I moved into the office a year and a half before. I took in the scenic view outside my office window, the Mississippi River just a few hundred feet away. I looked at my watch, took a deep breath, and headed across the building to my department chair's office.

My boss at "the U," as Minnesotans call it, was Professor Jim Hearn, a gentleman scholar who embodied the best aspects of his Southern roots. About eighteen months before that January morning, Jim offered me a tenure-track position in the College of Education and Human Development pending the completion of my doctorate. I had spent the previous four years in the University of Michigan's doctoral program in educational administration and policy and I was eager to leave the status of student and finally draw a real salary as faculty member at a Big Ten institution. I had readily accepted Jim's offer. Because I hadn't completed all my academic obligations at Michigan, the terms of my contract gave me two years to finish my doctorate and launch my academic career, a common arrangement for Ph.D. candidates taking academic positions.

I started the doctoral program at Michigan in 1995 after working at a Catholic high school for six years. As soon as I arrived in Ann Arbor, I jumped into the graduate student experience. I loved the intellectual challenge and the fast friends I made in the School of Education, not to mention my season tickets to Michigan football and hockey games.

Through the first two years in graduate school – mainly coursework – I made good progress, earned solid grades, and received lots of positive feedback from my professors. I started to look forward to the day when my own students would address me as "Professor Matheney."

My fledgling academic career was nurtured by my doctoral program advisor, Cecil Miskel. Cecil was the Dean of the Ed School for my first two years in Ann Arbor. Widely respected in educational administration circles, Cecil was known for his directness, sharp intellect, and the hint of an accent from his native Oklahoma.

Cecil provided me with a position on his research project, encouraged me to make presentations at conferences, involved me as a co-author of a published research article, and introduced me to prominent people in my field. He ensured that I had sufficient financial support for my doctoral studies. For a full-time graduate student, I had a great arrangement – my tuition was paid, and I had more income than many of my peers who were always looking for a class to teach or a research project to work on to pay the bills. Cecil was very good to me.

He was an important intellectual mentor as well. He taught me how to read research critically, and he critiqued my writing thoughtfully. Cecil instilled in me a very disciplined, analytical approach to thinking.

But late in my third year of graduate school, I realized that both my motivation and my relationship with Cecil were beginning to suffer. Despite small signs that things weren't going well – he was growing increasingly frustrated with one small project I led – I still managed to meet all of my doctoral program requirements except for the dissertation and became a Ph.D. candidate.

I found, however, that my modest enthusiasm for my dissertation topic – applying theoretical models to state education policymaking – was becoming more problematic. Deep in my heart, I knew I wasn't pursuing my passion. As a researcher, I wanted to be immersed in the culture of schools, observing principals, teachers and students. I wanted to be "in the field" elbow-to-elbow with students, teachers and principals. I enjoyed my studies of the politics of education, but my passion was much more evident when I thought about looking at schools through a cultural lens. I felt the lure of the kind of research done by another Ed School mentor, Loren "Biff" Barritt. Biff had spent a year immersed in a Dutch elementary school, studying the interactions of teachers and students.[4]

My interest in research through a cultural lens flourished when I took a class taught by Ruth Behar, the cultural anthropologist and McArthur genius grant recipient. A novice to cultural anthropology, I found that Ruth's teaching and the books we read deeply resonated with me. I felt a strong intellectual kinship to the authors we read.

The dissonance I experienced as a result of Ruth's class didn't go away. My heart continued to draw me in a different direction. I knew, though, that pursuing a very different path for my research involved considerable risk. If I left Cecil's research project to pursue my own interests, I'd lose the financial support that it provided. I'd have to find another source of income to support my doctoral studies, and money was already tight. After six years of subsistence salaries in Catholic education, I had no savings to fall back on. I had neither the guts nor the financial wherewithal to make a change. I was trapped by the graduate school equivalent of "golden handcuffs."

During my fourth and final year in Ann Arbor, the signs of trouble in my academic life multiplied. I was distracted by some developments in my personal life, and my lack of focus showed. I knew there were problems, and I think Cecil did too, but both of us avoided the topic. In one particular meeting with Cecil and another fellow graduate student, the tension was almost tangible. As the meeting progressed, he grew visibly impatient as I presented what he perceived to be mediocre work, and he wasn't entirely wrong. "This is an example of *bad* research," he said, with as much frustration and anger as I had ever seen from him.

Because of the warning signs, I thought briefly about returning to the university for a fifth year of graduate school. It would give me time to get back on the solid path I had known for most of my time in Ann Arbor. But, with Cecil's blessing, I ignored the cautionary voice in my head and started looking for a university

---

[4] *An Elementary School in Holland: Experiment in Practice* by Loren S. Barritt

faculty position, as many Ph.D. candidates do when they reached a similar stage in their doctoral studies. I was very fortunate to have interest from a few universities and eventually accepted Minnesota's offer. I left Michigan, hopeful that the new start would rejuvenate me personally and academically.

When I arrived in the Twin Cities, I threw myself into making it my new home, and, apart from the cruel winters, I loved it. The promise of my academic career and the new start drew Steve, my boyfriend at the time, to Minnesota as well. After he graduated from Michigan, he chose to join me in Minneapolis and start his career there.

While our social life and my teaching flourished, work on my dissertation did not. I continued to lack passion for the research. Month after month, I didn't touch the files that were so important to my new academic career. My relationship with Cecil grew more aloof as evidence of my lack of motivation mounted.

With each passing day, I felt the clock counting down the two-year timeline Minnesota had given me to finish my doctoral work. Steve grew more concerned as my second year at "the U" approached the mid-year point. With my dissertation a total bust, the darkness of my reality was setting in.

After spending a moment in my office that bitter January morning, I checked in with Jim's secretary a few minutes early and took a seat outside his office. I had rehearsed what I would say to him a number of times in my head. Typically calm under pressure, I was unusually anxious as I waited for our meeting to begin. This conversation was unlike any I had in some time – maybe ever.

As I waited for Jim, my mind raced. I thought of all that had happened in my life since I left Ann Arbor to head west. In the fall of 1999, I had jumped into my new position at the U with eagerness. I developed a new syllabus for the Educational Foundations class I was to teach, one that typically wasn't very popular with prospective teachers. My syllabus and my instructional approach were a bit different than the usual fare at Minnesota. I focused on themes like equity and excellence in education, while trying to make the content practical to future classroom teachers. The results were very positive; my students gave the class and my teaching high ratings. I took great pride in the impact I was having.

My thoughts were interrupted when Jim, always punctual, peaked out his door at the appointed time and waved me inside his office.

"Have a seat. Hey, I wanted to mention all the good things I hear about your teaching. Your students really love your classes," he said.

"Thanks. My students are great. I'm feeling really good about the classes." I said, pausing, not really eager to move on with the conversation.

Jim pushed gently, "But I think we have other agenda items today, right?"

"Yes." I paused again. "Jim, I want to thank you for everything. You've been really good to me. Really patient." I swallowed hard. "But we both know this isn't going to work out. I'm sorry." I started to choke on my words. Though I had practiced what I wanted to say, getting them out wasn't easy.

I composed myself for a second or two. "You've invested a lot in me, but I'm not going to be able finish my doctorate on time. I'm not going to make the deadline. I'm going to have to resign." The taste of the word "resign" lingered in the back of my throat.

So much of my self-esteem was wrapped up in my identity as an education scholar. Since I was five years old, school was *my* thing. I had just admitted to Jim that I was a failure at the very thing that the important people in my life thought I did best. I knew I had to resign or inevitably get fired in a few months for failing to complete my Ph.D.

And there I was, meeting that January morning with my department chair to share my decision. Though the lesser part of me wanted to blame Cecil, I knew I couldn't. I knew what I had to do, but I had failed at something that was deeply important to me. I had failed at achieving one of the most important goals I had ever set out for myself. I had failed Steve, Cecil, and my supportive colleagues at the U. I had disappointed many people who believed in me and looked up to me.

Jim's response to my decision was predictably magnanimous.

"I'm sorry, too. I knew things weren't going well. I don't want you to feel any shame about this. In the short time you've been here, you've done a great job with your classes – be proud of that."

"Thanks. That means a lot, but I still feel terrible."

"I know things will turn out alright. Any ideas about what's next for you?"

"I've been talking it over with Steve. I'd like to teach my last two classes here and work on my principal's license. I'll look for an administrative job when that's wrapped up. I let Steve down, and I owe it to him to make something of this."

"Let me know how I can help," Jim said, as we began to talk about the logistics of my departure.

Five months after that meeting, I taught my last class at the U and turned in my grades. Wulling Hall was empty on my last day there – it was a Friday afternoon on a college campus – so I didn't have to say any awkward good-byes. I didn't have a job lined up so I didn't have anything to tell people. I handed my office key to Jim's secretary. Then I loaded the last box of my books into the crappy used car I bought when I left Ann Arbor and headed home.

2002: Prior Lake, Minnesota. A couple weeks before the end of the school year on a clear June Wednesday, a young woman made her way to the assistant principal's office as she thought of everything she was looking forward to in the coming weeks – all the festivities surrounding the end of her high school career – the award ceremonies, the graduation parties, yearbook-signing, and even the Commencement itself for which she had earned the honor of speaking on behalf of her class. It had been a good senior year for Laura, and she was proud of what she achieved. She was one of leaders of the Class of 2002 and was going to attend college at one of her top choices. But, as is the case for ambitious adolescents, she put a lot of pressure on herself to achieve. Sometimes, amid the stresses of senior year, she appreciated taking a moment or two during the school day to catch her breath and spend a few minutes with a sympathetic set of ears.

With Graduation Day approaching, the young woman knocked on the door of the assistant principal's office at Prior Lake Senior High School, a school of 1,200 students on the edge of metropolitan Minneapolis and the Minnesota prairie. Waved into the office, where discipline forms and student schedules littered a small conference table, Laura took a seat and said cheerfully, "How's your day going?"

She wasn't a regular in the assistant principal's office – that was for certain. But the school secretaries knew Laura – who was poised and, as they would say, "put-together" – would stop by once in a while and politely ask to speak to the assistant principal. She'd go into the office, chat for a few minutes, and be quietly on her way. Unlike many students who traversed that path, the secretaries noted, there were never any nefarious reasons behind the visits.

As she took a seat in the Assistant Principal's Office, Laura began to chat about her plans for graduation and her final summer before college. Then her tone changed slightly.

"I just wanted to thank you for taking time to listen to me this year. You always said you had time, even though I know you're super busy. Sometimes I just needed a break. My parents are great – you know that – but everyone needs somebody else to talk to once in a while. You just listened. That's why I wanted you to have this." Laura handed me a flat, gift-wrapped box.

"Wow, I'm ummm . . .," I said, a lump growing in my throat, "well, surprised."

I didn't think I had done anything special for her. To be honest, I didn't remember most of what we'd talk about in those brief conversations in my office. I didn't think they were a big deal. I thought Laura was the one who was being kind to the rookie assistant principal.

As I slowly unwrapped Laura's gift, I was reminded of other boxes – boxes I packed alone in my office filled with books and neglected files that I had loaded ignominiously into my car on my last day at the U. So much in my life had changed. I lifted the lid of Laura's box to see a tie with diagonal stripes in the school's colors. "Thanks for listening," she said. "I thought you might want to wear that at Graduation."

Laura had reminded me that I had persevered and made an impact, even in my first year – even with a student I didn't realize I was helping.

Fifteen years later, I still wear that tie. What the time represents – Laura's kindness, the value of seemingly small gestures, and my strength and resilience – has sustained me through a variety of leadership challenges as an assistant principal to principal to state Department of Education official and most recently, to leading the Philadelphia Academy of School Leaders.

I spent two more years at Prior Lake as an assistant principal. It was there that I learned that I had good instincts in working with teenagers and parents on difficult issues. I had worked closely with a number of students who struggled to be successful in school, and many had made progress. The impact that I had at the high school, along with Laura's words and the blue and gold tie, helped me heal and move forward. I took Ernest Hemingway's words to heart: "The world breaks everyone, and afterward many are strong at the broken places." I realized I was far more resilient than I had imagined, and I had learned about school leadership in a deeper, more concrete way than I could have ever experienced in graduate school. That strength "at the broken places" is now a permanent part of my ability to persevere.

MINDSETS FOR PERSEVERANCE

Throughout my career, as I weathered significant storms like leaving the U or smaller trials that I've already forgotten, I've found that possessing two mindsets have particularly bolstered my ability to persevere:

- Accepting that hardship and uncertainty are inevitably part of life
- Acknowledging that progress toward our hopes and dreams is slow and deliberate

We'll explore each from a variety of perspectives – from military history to religion to high school sports.

Volatile and uncertain. Apart from students of military history and strategy, Army General Maxwell Thurman's legacy is largely unknown. He spent 37 years serving his country, including stints in Vietnam as an intelligence adviser and artillery commander. Upon his death in 1994, the *New York Times* referred to him as "a principal architect of the all-volunteer United States Army." General Thurman led the U.S. Army Recruiting Command in the post-Vietnam era that reframed the Army as an opportunity to "be all that you can be," instead of a last-ditch option for young people with no direction.

In 1989, the General was hand-picked by President George H.W. Bush to lead the U.S. Southern Command, where he led the effort to depose dictator Manuel Noriega during the U.S. invasion of Panama. Six years later leukemia ended his life. He earned both the Distinguished Service Medal and the Bronze Star. Throughout his distinguished career he was known for his discipline, demanding leadership, and strategic mind. From Vietnam, to strengthening the all-volunteer Army, to Panama, his career clearly afforded an array of opportunities to hone his views of an uncertain world.

Thurman's legacy persists perhaps most notably in his framing of the nature of combat, national defense, and homeland security. He is credited by one Army War College study with coining a phrase that's been applied to many settings beyond military strategy. The author of that document credits Thurman with describing combat environments as "volatile, uncertain, complex, and ambiguous" – now popularly known in military, business, and leadership contexts as VUCA. The apt acronym, which became especially popular after 9/11, has been applied to many contexts, and the message is clear: We live in an inherently confusing, unpredictable world. Army generals know this. CEOs understand it. High school principals experience VUCA, and so do my niece and her husband with a two-year-old and another on the way.

A VUCA mindset acknowledges that, despite our best preparation, things will go awry. This doesn't mean that we should stop planning; it just reminds us that we shouldn't be surprised when things go differently than we expect. With a VUCA mindset, we are more likely to remain calm in the face of volatility.

Ironically, as a high school principal, I often thought about VUCA on the quieter days of school. Knowing that the calm could be quickly disrupted, I tried to make progress on the normal work of a principal such as planning for the next school year or evaluating teachers. I knew that I had to use those windows of opportunity productively until VUCA returned. And it inevitably did in a large high school.

In my fantasy world, I would enjoy eavesdropping on a conversation between General Thurman and the Buddha. Though I'm far from a Buddhist scholar, I believe the concept of VUCA would resonate with the great teacher. The first of the Four Noble Truths in Buddhism is *dukkha*, which addresses the inherent pain, suffering, and impermanence of life. One of the three natures of *dukkha* is, in fact, the changeable nature of things. Yes, life is unpredictable and difficult, the military strategist and the sage might agree.

We might ascertain a similar understanding from this Zen Buddhist proverb:

> "Before enlightenment: Chop wood, carry water.
> After enlightenment: Chop wood, carry water."

This teaching has been interpreted to mean many things. It may point to being mindful when doing daily activities, or it may allude in a way to the VUCA mindset. Before we achieve enlightenment or knowledge or that promotion we want, we must work hard and do the "chores" that life requires of us. After achieving the goal we seek, we still face the harsh realities of life. We may be self-actualized or have the C-suite, but life, though perhaps different, is still imperfect and difficult. There's still wood to be chopped and water to be carried.

Denial. From my experience, it seems that those who deny the volatile and uncertain nature of the world are likely to be poor leaders – or not be leaders at all. Despite substantial evidence to the contrary, these individuals fail to accept that "shit happens." They are the proverbial ostriches with their head in the sand. When the unpredictability of the world impacts their spheres of influence, their mindset prevents them from responding well. Because they haven't learned that struggle is an inevitable part of life, they're poorly situated to deal with it.

As a high school principal, I watched a few well-intentioned parents try to insulate their sons and daughters from learning the reality that life can be hard. These were *not* the parents who raised legitimate concerns. These were the parents who, in denying our VUCA world, subconsciously undermined their children's opportunity to develop resilience. I remember an incident involving one freshman boy on a weekend sleepover with other friends. In the middle of the night, the "friends" shaved the freshman's head. The mother was desperately upset by the incident. She not only reported the issue to me even though it wasn't a school incident, but she also filed a police report. Regardless of whether the incident was traumatic for the young man, the mother missed out on the opportunity to focus her energies on framing the moment as an opportunity to grow more resilient. She missed an opportunity to show her son a better way to respond when our friends disappoint us.

I often got to view similar efforts that undermined resilience when the school's athletic teams were making pre-season cuts. For example, after one student was cut after tryouts for one team, a parent wrote a three-page letter to the school's athletic director. She accused the coach of using brutal language in denying a spot for her daughter on the team. What was that brutal language? "You are not on the level as the other athletes."

I knew the coach of that team well. He's a kind, gentle guy who enjoyed the vocal support of his athletes' parents. I also know he *really* hated cutting kids from the team, and he made every effort to keep as many students on the team as possible.

Later in the parent's letter – as happened far too often in issues involving high school sports – the parent made threats: "Maybe I need to take this to the court of public opinion, for the purpose of giving kids and parents a voice for when they feel let down and rejected by their school for wanting to be a part of a team." This was truly the wrong lesson for her daughter.

Fortunately, the majority of parents whose sons and daughters got cut handled it very differently. Maybe they urged them to practice harder and try out again next year. Or perhaps the parents encouraged sons and daughters to find another sport or activity they enjoyed.

Whether you're trying to make a high school athletic team or writing to create a fictional world that readers will enjoy, a VUCA mindset and a desire to learn from the struggles from life can strengthen desire and resolve. In her wise 2008 address at Harvard's graduation, *Harry Potter* author J.K. Rowling described her rocky path to becoming one of history's bestselling authors. Seven years after her own college graduation, "I had failed on an epic scale," she shared. "I was jobless, a lone parent, and as poor as it is possible to be in modern Britain, without being homeless." Just surviving the trials of her 20s, she learned in retrospect, ultimately strengthened her. "The knowledge that you have emerged wiser and strong from setbacks means that you are, ever after, secure in your ability to survive."

One step at a time. On the very same morning that Rowling gave her now-famous address at Harvard, D.J. Gregory followed pro golfer Paul Goydos' group at the Stanford St. Jude Championship in Memphis. As the thermometer climbed to the low 90s that day, the 30-year-old D.J. walked about five miles as golfer Boo Weekly earned a one-stroke lead by the end of the round.

While that may not seem a significant accomplishment, it was a good day for D.J. The tournament in Memphis was his 23rd of 2008. He had walked every hole of every tournament during the PGA tour which was about at its half-way point for the season. This was a remarkable achievement for any golf fan, but particularly impressive for D.J., each of whose steps was hindered by cerebral palsy.

D.J. was born ten weeks premature. In his book *Walking with Friends: An Inspirational Year on the PGA Tour*, he explained his condition. Born prematurely, D.J. writes, "my lungs were not fully developed, and during my time in the neonatal intensive care unit nurses put too much oxygen into my bod, which burst the capillaries in my brain that control my lower extremities." As a result, D.J.'s legs were so contorted that his feet almost pointed backward. His toes stacked on top of each other. Doctors didn't believe that D.J. would ever be able to walk. Only after five surgeries were his legs straight enough to stand on. Through his parents' encouragement and insistence and his own determination, D.J. finally managed to learn to walk with crutches, then two canes, and finally, after years, a single cane.

Though he was unable to play many sports as a kid, D.J. still became a rabid sports fan, and he particularly loved golf. He was determined to teach himself to play the sport. Eventually, he figured out a way to use a cane to stabilize himself and just one arm to swing the golf club.

In 2008 D.J., an avid fan of professional golf, decided to pursue a dream: He would walk every hole of every round of every event of the professional tour. Whether he realized it or not, he accepted the VUCA nature of his endeavor: There would be unpredictable weather. He'd face pain from blisters on his feet. He'd face fatigue from walking that people without CP wouldn't understand.[5] He faced the reality that walking, even with a cane, was difficult for him. His goal was to fall less than once a week.

"If I fall, I fall. It's just another challenge. I'm going to fall," he told ESPN. "It's just the way it is. I'm going to do it. So you know what – you get back up and you learn from your mistakes and you don't do it again."

Ultimately, he walked in a most inspiring way. Step by step he made progress to his goal. From January in Kapalua, Hawaii to November in Orlando. 3,256 holes of golf. 988 miles. 44 tournaments in 45 weeks. Yes, he fell, but only 29 times, many fewer than his goal at the beginning of the challenge. Even more importantly, along the PGA tour stops, he visited patients facing similar physical disabilities at places like the Walter Reed National Military Medical Center and the St. Jude Children's Research Hospital to express his support and share his experiences.

Persistence," D.J. wrote after the 2008 golf tour, "is the mortar that holds the bricks of life in place. And it is the persistent person who overcomes adversity and thrives again, no matter what he's been through."

Ultimately, his accomplishment was the result of a determined, deliberate effort. "I can do what anyone else can do," he says, "it just takes a little more time."

Like D.J. Gregory during his golf odyssey, legendary cycling coach Sir David Brailsford understands the deliberate nature of making progress toward a goal. Paraphrasing the Chinese philosopher Lao Tzu, Brailsford says, "You can walk a thousand miles – you can only do it a step at a time. But it doesn't take long before you've done quite a few steps." Currently General Manager of Team Sky, the British professional cycling group, Brailsford understood this from the moment he first joined the British national cycling team in 1998. He ultimately led the national team for 11 years and is widely credited with turning it into the preeminent international power.

Brailsford believes that by improving everything connected to racing – training regimens, bike design, athlete nutrition – even just

---

[5] A graduate school friend, Karl Christiansen, once told me that for people with CP every single step was like walking up stairs. He reminded himself of the challenges his daughter Sophie faced with CP by avoiding elevators whenever possible. I met Sophie when she was a smart, determined girl of eight. She's now a six-time equestrian gold medalist after brilliant performances at the London and Rio Paralympic Games in 2012 and 2016. You can learn more about her at sophiechristiansen.co.uk.

a little bit, gains would ultimately add up. "It doesn't matter how small the improvement. We're going to do it. We're going to energize each other, and we're going to create a culture which is about. . .continuous learning, continuous improvement," he told the London Business Forum. This process, known as the "aggregation of marginal gains," led the British cycling team to huge leaps in Olympic medals under his leadership. For three consecutive Olympic games – Beijing, London, and Rio – the British team has stood atop cycling medal counts.

After spending eight years as a principal, I joined the New Jersey Department of Education (NJDOE) to lead the implementation of the landmark teacher tenure reform law, the TEACH NJ Act. Though we never were graced with gold medals, the team I led at the NJDOE earned its own recognition. As a result of our careful, deliberate progress developing a new state educator evaluation system, we were awarded the Commissioner's Excellence Award by state education chief Christopher Cerf.

Our success was particularly noteworthy because what we achieved occurred in a very VUCA environment. Education policy stakeholders, including the state teachers' union, some special interest groups, and a few State Board members and state legislators tried to knock us off course. But we persisted toward our policy goals under the leadership of Commissioner Cerf.

In leading that amazing team at the NJDOE, just as I did at the high school, I reminded the staff, "It's a marathon, not a sprint." In other words, high-quality work required deliberate progress every day, step-by-step, and, most importantly, relationship-by-relationship. Achieving substantial goals as an organization isn't about a quick sprint followed by breaking the tape and waving the flag. It requires patient, consistent effort. If you want a role model for leading your organization forward, think D.J. Gregory, not Usain Bolt.

SEEING BEYOND THE STRUGGLES

Acknowledging that our journeys – personal and professional – can be trying and difficult and knowing that progress toward our goals is often slow and deliberate are certainly important mindsets that position us well to persevere. These realistic mindsets are critical, but not sufficient, to help us weather the storms. In my life, I've found three key approaches that have helped me see beyond the struggles:

- "Changing the lens" to strengthen perseverance
- Finding a mantra that shapes and reinforces how we see ourselves
- Participating in rituals that renew us

Changing the lens. On that January morning after I left my boss's office at the University of Minnesota, I was at one of the lowest moments of my life. I was disgusted by my failure and deeply uncertain about my future. I began to question the traits that I thought characterized my life: responsibility, hard work, self-discipline. I owed it to my boyfriend Steve and to myself to figure out a plan to move on. As I had told my department chair, I planned to work hard to earn my principal's license in Minnesota as quickly as possible then start applying for administrative positions. I had about five months to make it all happen before I was unemployed.

So I moved forward. As I took a graduate class in the principalship at the U and found a practicum placement, I focused on positive sentiments that propelled me forward. I "changed the lens" on how I viewed my immediate past and framed a message that inspired hope in my future. This is what I told myself:

There may have been many reasons why I failed to thrive in higher education – some I may not entirely understand – but I know I love schools, teaching, and working with teenagers. I know from experience that I'm a good leader with great patience. Pursuing an administrative position in a high school will enable me to help teachers get better and help students pursue their goals. This is noble and important work.

There were several key messages as I "changed the lens" that helped me move forward. First, it shifted my mindset off the "blame game." I acknowledged that something had gone wrong, but placing that blame on my University of Michigan advisor or even myself wasn't going to help. My new perspective also reminded me of some my positive qualities. Yes, I'm passionate about education. Yes, I am patient. Yes, I am a good leader.

Finally, I was reminded of the value of the work that I was pursuing.

The statement was honest and accurate – it didn't overinflate my abilities or make me the victim. It was just enough to help me move on. In those moments when I felt embarrassed or disappointed about my failure to earn my Ph.D. – even years later – I returned to the way I re-framed the situation.

Another example of changing the lens comes from a former colleague. Monica and her boyfriend Frank had been together for more than five years, but, she confided, it was apparent that the relationship was losing steam. She acknowledged that in the last year together both she and Frank had sought intimacy outside the relationship. After months of tension, Frank told her that he thought the relationship was over. Monica was devastated, but deep down she knew he was right. She told me she cried off and on for about two days, but knew she had to get herself together and take a step forward. She spent some time journaling about what she was going through. She read through what she wrote, and then summarized it in a few spare sentences that focused her on several key messages that would help her move forward:

> *I realize that my love for Frank has evolved. While I still have deep love and affection for him, our relationship must end. We are fortunate to have five years of great memories. I chose to be with Frank because of the qualities and character I recognized when we met. Those qualities haven't changed despite the end of our relationship. I'm saddened by our behavior at the end of our relationship, but we can best heal and move on by treating each other with love and respect.*

Through the moments of jealousy, anger, and sadness as they parted ways, Monica revisited her re-framing often. The sentiments her words expressed guided her forward. As it turns out, both Monica and Frank both lived up to the statement. They remain friendly and are now both in other loving relationships.

At their best, the process of re-framing challenges in our lives helps us grow toward, in Abraham Lincoln's words, "the better angels of our nature." When we experience struggles, we want to be petty and play the blame game: "It's my dissertation advisor's fault I didn't finish." "Our marriage would've lasted if my spouse had been more (insert quality here)." Changing the lens helps us make sense of our unpredictable lives while keeping us honest and moving us forward.

Mantras. Leaders have long tried to motivate their subordinates by using a pithy phrase. New England Patriots football coach Bill Belichick is famous for repeatedly reminding his players to "Do your job." As he led Apple and Pixar, Steve Jobs returned often to the words on the back of the *Whole Earth Catalog*: "Stay Hungry, Stay Foolish." Aubrey Newman, then a colonel in the U.S. Army, is credited with the simple injunction "Follow me!" when commanding a regiment leading General Douglas MacArthur's famous return to the Philippines during World War II.

Some of these mantras catch on for decades. "Follow me" remains a popular infantry slogan, for example, with the words emblazoned on the Army Infantry School uniform patch.

In the tradition of Belichick, Jobs, and Newman, I have similarly used mantras to motivate others and myself when presented with leadership challenges.

As I showered before work on September 16, 2008, a few days after the start of my fifth year as a principal at South Brunswick High School, I heard this ominous introduction from my morning news source:

"This is Morning Edition from NPR News. . . . I'm Steve Inskeep. We're spending a good deal of this morning trying to figure out one thing. It's the economy; what's going wrong . . . and . . . how much we really need to worry. In this part of the program, we begin with the Wall Street firms whose trouble knocked more than 500 points off the Dow Jones Industrials yesterday. Lehman Brothers is bankrupt, the giant insurance company AIG is in trouble, and federal officials are trying to figure out what to do."

Though far from being an expert, I knew enough as a former economics teacher that our nation faced serious days ahead. A few local employers had already made layoffs, and I knew that a number of families in our community were already hurting from the early days of the recession.

Throughout the next year, I saw mom-and-pop stores in the community struggle, and I knew of families buried by unaffordable mortgages. The tax base in the township was deteriorating under the weight of the economic downturn. Within a year of that NPR story, state revenues had fallen precipitously, which resulted in reduced state funding of public schools. Meanwhile, the district's fixed costs driven by contracts with its employees continued to rise. As Superintendent Gary McCartney reminded us many times in the coming months, we needed to "prepare for the worst and hope for the best."

As the impact of the bad economy continued, we faced significant cuts for the 2010-11 school year, the worst year for districts across the nation during the Great Recession. By the time we prepared a budget, we had eliminated more than 15 teaching positions, eliminated the positions of three well-liked supervisors, laid off a guidance counselor, social worker, and a nurse. We reduced the hours of nearly every hall and cafeteria monitor, many of whom lived paycheck to paycheck. And we eliminated many paid extracurricular and coaching positions. The staff members who were fortunate to keep their jobs faced increased workloads. As the school year ended in June 2010, it was a difficult time as teachers said goodbye to colleagues who wouldn't be returning to jobs in the fall.

During the summer of 2010, I prepared to start the new school year under the "new normal." I thought about what I could say to staff members who were experiencing the pain of sacrifice and disruption. I wrestled with different tones – inspirational, emotional, or perhaps motivational. In the end I settled on five words. As they settled in for our first meeting before the school year began I told them, "It's a hard hat year." That sentence acknowledged that these were difficult times for many people we cared about, but we needed to hunker down and get down to the work that mattered so much to us – teaching kids. We were going to be focused on the essential, face the "new normal," and persevere despite smaller budgets and fewer teachers.

Once the school year started, I revisited the mantra at the next faculty meeting. I explained to the staff that I wanted to recognize colleagues who are models of perseverance at our meetings throughout the year. We'd honor those people who "put on their hard hats and get down to work." At that point, from behind the podium I pulled out a couple of purchases from the dollar store – plastic hard hats emblazoned with stickers of the school logo. It was an inexpensive, fun way to revisit the message and honor some great role models.

I also used the mantra to re-orient the staff when we got off track. Sometimes teachers would complain about some of the smaller problems resulting from the cutbacks. I'd respond by acknowledging their frustration and reminding them how lucky we were. "Remember, it's a hard hat year. You and I are lucky to still have jobs. We have to make the most of what we have."

Most of them responded well to the message: "Okay, you're right. I get it."

While the mantra and the "hard hat" awards didn't solve all the morale problems that resulted from layoffs and cutbacks, I know that many teachers appreciated that I was acknowledging how challenging those days were.

Some leadership trials have a wide organizational impact like the Great Recession. Many people were affected in the high school, and the "hard hat" approach helped, in a small way, to focus our persistence through layoffs and cutbacks. At other times, tests of leadership are more personal in nature. I experienced a few moments like that when I felt my leadership was under a more intense spotlight than usual. One time it was a self-inflicted wound when I didn't think of all the repercussions of a decision; another was a series of bomb threats that were disrupting school one spring. Through all those moments of intense scrutiny, I was buoyed by the mantra "I am a warrior."

"I am a warrior" means many things to me. It meant I'm stronger than the circumstances that confront me. It means I've been tested before by life's struggles and survived – even thrived. It means I'm not a victim. A good personal mantra points me to qualities that I need to hear: I am strong. I persevere.

And so, I've repeated the mantra in my head many times as I head into a difficult meeting or feel my energy for "battle" wane. On the most difficult days, I even repeat the mantra in my head at the gym, sweating off the stress of the day.

There are moments, too, when I say the mantra as a form of celebration. I recall presiding at one Graduation in the midst of many stressors in my personal life. My brief remarks to graduates went well, and the students were respectful throughout the ceremony. It had been a very upbeat, positive afternoon. With the final student's name read and the last diploma handed over, I repeated the words silently to myself: I am a warrior.

Rituals. 2016 wasn't an easy year for me. My partner Ken and I moved (entirely by ourselves) from our home in New Jersey to Philadelphia at the start of the year. My father passed away in March. And I was leading a non-profit startup with sky-high expectations. It was also the year I would turn 50.

As my birthday approached, Ken asked what I wanted to do to celebrate. I had never been a fan of big birthday parties, even as a child. When my parents asked me what I wanted to do on my birthday as a youngster, I'd opt for a night out at my favorite restaurant at the time, the Toledo landmark Tony Packo's. Even today, I can speak comfortably in front of thousands of people, but I'd prefer to not be the center of attention at a party. I've tried to skip the ritual of the birthday party as often as possible, and I'd been pretty successful at it.

But for the first time in many years, Ken and I decided that my friends and family wouldn't let me get away with that for my 50th and planned a party. My nieces and nephew flew in for the weekend as did my cousin Mark from Chicago. Friends came from the Jersey Shore, New York, and points in between. After dinner at my favorite restaurant, we hosted a soccer-themed party at our apartment. Our friend and bartender Anthony, clad in a soccer kit, served signature cocktails (the "MVP" and the "Benchwarmer" were quite popular), and people were amazed at the three-tiered cake adorned at the top with an edible soccer ball. We had gone all out, and it was a great night.

At one point during the party, I paused just to look at my assembled friends and family. I saw my far-flung family members talking to the folks from New Jersey and Philly like they were long-lost friends. These important people from different stages in my life were celebrating together. I was humbled by their presence and affection. I was proud of the loving, smart, and funny people who were part of my life. I was reminded, despite the challenges of the year, of how many people had my back. For days that followed, I felt like I was being projected forward by the love that I experienced that night. I was reminded by the deep connections I had with all of the loved ones present – and even those who couldn't make it. After a challenging year, I was energized and hopeful.

The ritual of the birthday party was never that important to me, but that 50th celebration taught me something new. Rituals – like the ones where the most important people in our lives come together – remind us of how much we're loved. They remind us what our values are.

Many of us are familiar with rituals, both religious and secular, that remind us of the value of perseverance. The story of the Israelites' Exodus from Egypt told at the Passover Seder is a reminder of the resolve of the Jewish people. For many Christians, the light of the Paschal candle at the Easter vigil is a reminder of hope after the darkness of Good Friday. Many schools now hold celebrations on the 100th day of the school year, celebrating what students have accomplished to that point and generating excitement for the learning in the days ahead. Celebrating the 100th day reminds students of the value and purpose of the important work they do in school every day.

In one of the most anticipated rituals before a sporting event anywhere in the world, the New Zealand Men's National Rugby Team – known for decades as the All Blacks – takes an aggressive formation near the middle of the field. Eyes bulging and voice straining, one member of the team begins a chant in the language of the indigenous people of New Zealand, the Maori. As the choreographed tribal dance proceeds, teammates stamp their feet and join the rhythmic chanting in the Maori language:

Hi aue, hi! Ko Aotearoa e ngunguru nei!
This is our land that rumbles

Au, au, aue ha!
And it's my time! It's my moment!

Ko Kapa o Pango e ngunguru nei!
This defines us as the All Blacks[6]

---

[6] From *Kapo a pango*, a *haka* written specifically for the All Blacks in 2005.

As the mesmerizing ritual continues, the team crouches and menacingly slaps their hands against their forearms and thighs. They glare at their opponents who typically stand in a line just beyond mid-field returning the stare.

It's one of the most exciting team rituals in the world. The *haka* adds to the mystique of the All Blacks, who are the preeminent power in international rugby. They are consistently ranked first in the world and have won the last two Rugby World Cups (2011 and 2015).

The *haka* epitomizes a ritual. "A ritual," explained scholar Joseph Campbell, "is the enactment of a myth." Rituals, by participating in them, connect us to the wisdom and purpose they represent. The All Blacks are reminded of their purpose as warriors on the rugby field and their ability to persevere in a brutal sport.

Personal narratives, mantras, and rituals all serve as mental roadmaps for perseverance. They remind us of the values and strengths that enable us to persist, and they provide us with a pathway forward.

PURPOSE AND PERSEVERANCE

> "If we have our own why of life,
> we shall get along with almost any how."
> – Friedrich Nietzsche, philosopher

Whether it's expressed by changing the lens, repeating a mantra, or performing a ritual, having a strong sense of purpose or mission is a critical aspect of perseverance. For example, the All Blacks' *haka* connects the team deeply to their purpose – representing their people with courage and ferocity in battle – just as it did for their Maori ancestors. It's the deeply-rooted purpose that enables the All Blacks to achieve unrivaled success. Having a strong "why," represented in the *haka* or in some other way, enables us to find a way forward.

I appealed to the deep sense of purpose educators share as the Great Recession impacted the high school. I knew that many staff members had been impacted by the economic slowdown, and as the winter holidays approached one year I needed to acknowledge this.

In an email I sent to the staff before winter break, I wrote, "Despite the personal and professional challenges that confronted many of us in 2010, I remain steadfastly optimistic. Unlike so many adults, you and I get to wake up in the morning knowing that we are doing something profoundly important."

"Having a strong sense of purpose in life," I continued, "creates for us the best foundation for persevering through difficult times."

Long walks and long goodbyes. Holding the deepest sense of purpose enabled Nelson Mandela to survive 27 years of imprisonment. As President of post-Apartheid South Africa, he led a national reconciliation that quite likely prevented a civil war and preserved the nation. Shortly after being elected President, Mandela beautifully captured the nature of perseverance in his memoir *Long Walk to Freedom*.

> "I have discovered the secret that after climbing a great hill, one only finds that there are many more hills to climb. I have taken a moment here to rest, to steal a view of the glorious vista that surrounds me, to look back on the distance I have come. But I can rest only for a moment, for with freedom comes responsibilities, and I dare not linger, for my long walk is not yet ended."

Mandela's purpose – his "long walk" – propelled him forward, hill after hill. In his artful prose, he encourages us to understand the arduous nature of life's journey, the value of rest and reflection, and the importance of knowing when to return to the challenges we confront, for our "long walk is not yet ended."

A few months after my mother turned 69, my father received a phone call from a longtime friend of the family. For decades, she and my mother had been members of a Bunco Club, whose eight members gathered monthly to play a dice game.

"Dean," my mother's friend, who was a nurse, gently began, "I'm a little concerned about Bettie. I think you should get her checked out by a neurologist."

"What do you think is wrong?" My dad asked.

"At our last club, I noticed she had some problems following the game. Doing simple math. You know that's not like her. I think it might be dementia or Alzheimer's."

My dad wasn't overly surprised by the call. He had noticed little signs, as had my brother and I, but all three of us had chalked it up to just Mom getting a little older. With this additional opinion from a friend who'd known our mother so long, Dad decided to take her to the doctor. It started with some simple tests in the doctor's office that raised concerns. That was followed by an MRI that indicated my mother was, in fact, suffering from dementia, possibly related to some heart and vascular problems that she had experienced. The condition had probably been progressing for a year or so.

For much of the first year after the diagnosis, my father shielded me from the progression of the disease. I was in my second year as a principal, and he didn't want me to worry. In reality, it was a very difficult year. My mother, growing in frustration as her mental impairments increased, acted out. Always a fastidious homemaker, she scratched walls with pencils and pens in frustration. She uncharacteristically yelled at my father and even took swings at him, though she never hurt him physically.

As my mother's "long goodbye" progressed, her aggression fortunately faded. By the second year and third years of her diagnosis, she became more and more childlike. She constantly needed reassurance and attention.

After spending a few days with my parents on one of my trips to their home in Ohio, I told my dad I needed to do some "work stuff" and headed to a local coffee shop. I needed a few minutes' break from listening to my mother ramble on about nothing in particular. In my journal that day, I recorded some thoughts about perseverance, marriage, and the nature of commitment:

"What do marriage vows mean? What does 'Til death do you part' really mean. It's pleasant and quaint in the atmosphere of a cozy church with two 20-somethings standing at the altar. 'Yes, we'll be loyal forever. We'll take care of each other forever.' Does that mean forever as in 'when cancer ravishes my spouse' or 'when dementia forces me to care for a spouse who babbles like a five-year-old'? I look at what my father does. He answers to the questions "Where are you,

Dean?" and "How're you doing, honey?" dozens of times a day. He has to change the bed linens frequently because sometimes the diaper doesn't help. He makes sure my mother bathes and eats and takes her medicine.

Occasionally Dad gets a little time to himself to go to the barbershop or run a few errands. When Mom is napping he'll escape by reading a book about World War II. Those are his few respites from answering the same questions over and over.

When you think about courage, you think about someone commanding a military unit taking fire or a fireman running into a house consumed with flames. You don't think about courage to wake up every morning to a confused wife, tearing urine-stained sheets and blankets from the bed, starting the first of several loads of laundry, and facing a day filled with nonsense singing, the same questions over and over, and the slow mental demise of someone you have spent nearly 50 years with.

I lived with my mother's condition for six days and found my patience tried. I had bad dreams during the week when I rarely if ever do so at home. I faced the reality of the day when my mother recedes further into childlike behavior and ultimately no longer recognizes me. My father lives with those realities every day. And he faces those realities well – my father lovingly provides for my mother. For a man who did little housework for most of his life, he's now the caretaker in so many ways. He represents the daily heroism of so many people who face this reality every day."

Because of my mother's illness, my parents' life together took an uncertain, sometimes volatile turn, but Dad persevered because of a profound sense of purpose. My father always had a strong belief in fulfilling one's duty, and during Mom's illness he spoke often of his wedding vows. They were much more than a mantra to him. He saw his responsibilities through the lens of the pledge he made on April 11, 1959, and he would fulfill that promise. But much more importantly, his purpose and perseverance were rooted in his great love and devotion for her across more than 50 years.

Despite the trials, my father never wavered. He fulfilled his commitment until my mother's own "long walk" ended. On that day in 2010, with Dad and many family members at her side, she died peacefully and deeply loved.[7]

---

[7] Sadly, a few years after my mother's death, her sister – my beloved Aunt Myrna – was also diagnosed with dementia. As he cares for her, my Uncle Dave is the same kind of role model of love, compassion and perseverance as my father was.

CHAPTER SIX

THRIVE

Summer evenings in our Midwestern home in the early 1980s were usually pretty quiet. My brother, five years older, had a job, his own friends, and his own schedule. So more often than not it was just Mom, Dad, and me. Mom would put out dinner between 5:30 and 6:00, and we'd discuss how our day went or the news in our small town. After dessert – and there was always dessert – we'd tag team on loading the dishwasher before watching the news on TV.

We were an NBC family. I grew up on David Brinkley, John Chancellor, and their successors. On one early summer day in 1982 – I was 15, a rising high school sophomore – Dad turned the TV on at 6:30 as we took our respective positions. Dad took the armchair, Mom the La-Z-Boy rocker, and I sprawled out on the couch.

A few minutes into the broadcast, a young Tom Brokaw introduced a story with the words "Cancer Study" over his right shoulder. In his distinctive baritone, Brokaw read, "Scientists at the National Centers for Disease Control in Atlanta today released the results of a study which shows that the lifestyle of some male homosexuals has triggered an epidemic of a rare form of cancer. Robert Bazell now in Atlanta."

Then, Bazell, the NBC science reporter, began his report:

"Bobby Campbell of San Francisco and Billy Walker of New York both suffer from a mysterious, newly-discovered disease, which affects mostly homosexual men. But it has also been found in heterosexual men and women. The condition severely weakens the body's ability to fight disease."

While the *New York Times* had first reported on AIDS a year earlier, news of the nascent epidemic only reached small towns like mine through the news stories like this one.

At the time of that report, I was an honor roll student, involved in activities at my all-boys Catholic high school, and an obedient, religious son who caused no trouble. But, while it was impossible for me to put words to it at that age, I was experiencing a serious internal struggle, torn between who I thought I might be and who my world wanted me to be. I thought I might be gay.

It didn't make sense to me at the time. I didn't feel a connection to the few LGBT people who were visible in 1982. Though out-of-the-closet celebrities in the early '80s like Billie Jean King, Harvey Fierstein, and Elton John had admirable traits, they were not role models who resonated with the 15-year-old version of myself, a low-key kid with three passions: baseball, politics, and books. This attraction was distinct from any other element of my identity.

Any possibility that I was gay was pushed further away as the media, increasingly covering the AIDS story through 1982, seemed to equate being gay with illness or death. As a kid interested in the news, I heard the reports time and time again in my high school years and for many years to come. The result was a sense that it might never be possible to act on an important part of myself.

But I was a bit more fortunate than many LGBT kids entering their teenage years in 1980. Ours was a pretty civil home. Blatant slurs against any group of people were not a part of what it meant to be a good Christian. In my entire life, for example, I never heard either of my parents use the word "faggot." Of course, there were some not-so-subtle messages: My dad mentioned a few times that he thought one of his colleagues was "light in the loafers" and that his marriage was a sham. On several occasions as I grew up, he also shared a story from his college years. His parents heard rumors that the owner of a boarding house where my father was living was "homosexual." "My parents drove as fast as they could to Bowling Green, packed up my stuff, and got me out of there," he recalled. The stories reinforced the prevailing stereotypes: Gay men were shamed, effeminate, and predatory.

In high school – even later in college – being me took a lot of effort. I worked so hard to fit into the heteronormative world of that time. I was so concerned that something I wore, how I walked, or how I crossed my legs made me look gay. It was from this experience that I first learned how to compartmentalize my life. While my straight high school classmates were exploring relationships with girls, I sealed my desire for intimacy in a dark, tight box. It remained sealed for years with significant implications for my well-being.

As it is for many teens, I found "fitting in" during high school difficult for other reasons, too. I was a bookish, introverted kid, who lived a good distance from my high school. The geography made building strong friendships harder. Other students started at the high school with established groups of friends from their public and Catholic grade schools, while I knew no one the first day of my freshman year. It took a while to find my niche.

I don't know what would have happened to me as an isolated teen struggling with his deepest fears if I hadn't found a strong sense of purpose in school activities. The high school newspaper staff was particularly important. Tom Harms, our advisor, made certain that our office was a safe place for kids who didn't always fit in elsewhere in the school. Tom nurtured my developing leadership skills, and I felt that I could – almost – be entirely myself in that office.

With the newspaper, other activities, and my heavy academic load, I stretched myself too thin. I missed days of school from exhaustion and stress. Sometimes I would just tell my parents I had a stomach ache so I could stay home. On those days, I needed a respite from the achiever version of myself. I felt overwhelmed by my responsibilities, expectations, and personal burdens. I never let anyone know though. I couldn't let anyone see that weakness.

As I moved on to Princeton, the idea that I was gay remained difficult for me to fathom, and Princeton in the late 1980s was not a good place to figure it out. In almost any group of college guys of that era, gay jokes were common, and even at Princeton, out students were often the subject of ridicule. Despite being very involved in campus life, I personally knew no openly LGBT students.

My journal from those years revealed my struggle. When I was 19, I wrote, "I feel myself struggling now. . .trying to tell myself 'no.' You don't feel that way," and in a later entry, "My feelings have not subsided. Nothing has changed."

As I did in high school, my schoolwork and my activities at Princeton were my coping mechanism. I threw myself into college life and survived because of a large group of friends and the joys I found in getting a great education.

By my senior year, however, my emotional isolation and lack of intimacy were stifling. Despite my friends, a research project I loved, and significant extracurricular responsibilities, I felt profound loneliness, even when surrounded by people I cared for. I was forced to face the fact that, despite many prayers on my knees in the Princeton Chapel, being gay was an unchangeable part of me. Just beginning to say it to myself was a tentative, freeing step forward.

Despite that tentative step, because of circumstances and choice, I still continued to compartmentalize after Princeton. My only job offer in the teaching profession a month after graduation was from my alma mater, the Catholic high school in Toledo, clearly not an ideal environment for resolving a struggle over sexual orientation.

I continued my previous patterns, ignored my internal realities, and threw myself into the job. I distracted myself by spending long hours preparing for my classes and advising the yearbook staff, which turned out to be one of the best leadership experiences of my life. At least professionally, that approach to survival worked for about three years. There was so much about the job I loved. I loved teaching my government classes, and I was good at it. I made great friends among the faculty, and I really enjoyed my students.

But during my fourth year, my feelings were getting harder to ignore. I heard priests talk at Mass about the "fullness of life" and knew that phrase didn't describe mine. While my friends went on dates or spent time with their spouses, I worked late at school and came home to an empty apartment and an answering machine with no messages. Something had to change. I couldn't continue on like this.

In the coming months, I started to come out to some trusted family and friends. I came out to my first college friend on a subway in Manhattan. It went well. Then I told my socially liberal aunt and uncle. They, too, said all the right things. One by one, I told the most important people in my life. When I finally told my parents some time later, they too expressed their acceptance, love and support. With each conversation, I felt my confidence grow. I was revealing the real me.

Around the same time, I started to think about other career options – being openly gay and working in an all-boys Catholic school wasn't a good fit at the time. As a first step toward another possible career, I accepted a position in the school's Development Office, handling annual giving and alumni relations. I figured I'd spend a couple of years doing that, and then move to a city with more opportunities for me personally and professionally.

As part of that transition, I was sent to what was essentially a fundraising "boot camp" in San Francisco. One evening after our class, needing some time to work through all thoughts swirling in my head, I walked for miles through the city. I saw gay and lesbian people being themselves and gay couples walking hand-in-hand.

When I finally reached the Castro neighborhood, I saw, first-hand, the realities of the AIDS epidemic. I saw AIDS patients leaning on the love of friends. One very ill man was just angles and bones, pushed in a wheelchair. Another walked slowly with a cane, chatting amiably with a friend. One, I'll never forget, was marked by the lesions of Kaposi sarcoma. It was the summer of 1993. AIDS-related deaths in the U.S. would not peak for another two years.

In that walk through the Castro, I saw signs of a community decimated by epidemic, but still caring for its people and pushing on. Healthy or ill, the men I saw that evening were examples of vulnerability and strength. I was inspired by their love – their ferocity to be themselves. I, too, needed to be vulnerable and strong.

"Happiness," Mahatma Gandhi said, "is when what you think, what you say, and what you do are in harmony." Coming out was an essential step toward experiencing that kind of harmony in my life. Learning to be happy – to thrive – involves many steps in many different parts of your life. In this chapter, we'll explore four aspects of that long journey. The first three concepts may be familiar: Authenticity, vulnerability, and gratitude. The fourth, which focuses on turning toward the essentials in life, I term "living close to the core."

AUTHENTICITY

"To be nobody-but-yourself — in a world which is doing its best,
night and day, to make you everybody else — means to fight the
hardest battle which any human being can fight;
and never stop fighting."
– E. E. Cummings, "A Poet's Advice to Students"

Two years after that walk in the Castro, I left my work in the
high school – not for another development job, but for graduate
school at the University of Michigan. From the moment I stepped
foot in Ann Arbor as a graduate student, I was finally fully and
completely out, and I felt more whole than I ever had in my life.
By today's standards, I'd be considered a late bloomer. But as soon
as I came out, I never closeted myself again. Despite the
temptations of the convenience of the closet – especially when
you're an educator – I insisted on never turning back. If I were to
thrive as a person and a leader, I had to be totally me.

The many years I wasn't comfortable with my true self
certainly had two significant implications. First, adolescence and
young adulthood are challenging enough without putting so much
energy into denial and hiding. The energy that goes into
maintaining the closet is diverted from much more productive
pursuits – from achieving one's full potential. While I'm proud of
what I accomplished in my closeted years, I know I could have
been happier and more fulfilled if I didn't have to focus on hiding
my authentic self.

The second implication is the set of consequences we
experience when we are denied healthy forms of love and affection.
Closeted gay men of my generation often sought relief from the
burdens of the closet in addictions and dishonest and unhealthy
relationships. Perfectionism was one way that I sought escape.

Living or working in a culture that impedes authenticity has
expansive impacts, as Dr. Zhivago explains in Boris Pasternak's
classic novel:

"The great majority of us are required to live a life of constant,
systematic duplicity. Your health is bound to be affected if, day
after day, you say the opposite of what you feel, if you grovel

before what you dislike and rejoice at what bring you nothing but misfortune. Our nervous system isn't just a fiction, it's part of our physical body, and our soul exists in space and is inside us, like teeth in our mouth. It can't be forever violated with impunity."

Over time, a life of "systematic duplicity" erodes the most important elements of ourselves.

Fortunately, I survived my duplicity as did a majority of my peers from that era. We came out on our own timelines and achieved the authenticity that had eluded us. Through the bravery of LGBT people born in the 1960s and 70s – and those who came before us – teenagers and college students today are much less burdened by the problems of identity my peers and I struggled with. I'm proud to be part of the legacy of authenticity that we shared with them.

While the struggle to be truly oneself is, in Cummings' words, "the hardest battle any human being can fight," I know that that process of growth shaped me in significant ways. My own pursuit of wholeness has enabled me to recognize that struggle in others – especially the teenagers I worked with. My struggle to be honest with myself and others helped me to become a better leader.

My greatest dream as a principal – the one that I believed would transform the school and the lives of the people within it – has its roots in authenticity. I dreamt of a safe and trusting environment where everyone, adults and students alike, set aside their masks as they walked through the front doors of school. I dreamt of students unencumbered by expectations of sexual orientation, religion, differing levels of ability, gender, and race, driven only by their desire to do well and care for others.

I wanted the three-sport athlete intrigued enough by theater to try out for the musical.

I wanted the kid with five Advanced Placement classes to find out she loved sculpture.

I wanted the student whose family has faced eviction and bare shelves not to feel shame.

In my eight years as a principal, we took a few giant steps toward this vision, but there was still a work to be done.

Whether it's a school, a company, or athletic team, when people let down their defenses — where they know they can be authentic — their minds, bodies, and souls are less burdened. They are able to channel more energy into the work that really matters. In an environment that cultivates trust, leaders have to spend less time negotiating the conflict that results from inauthenticity and can focus more on leading important work. They can lead healthy teams where members are honest with each other and conflict over ideas and solutions is productive.

VULNERABILITY

As about 30 teachers trailed into a classroom, they chatted amiably about weddings attended, relaxing weeks at the New Jersey Shore, and new babies on the way. It was the usual chitchat of teachers getting back together after the two months of summer break. The teachers had just started a few days of meetings in preparation for the beginning of the 2011-12 school year, my eighth year of leading South Brunswick High School.

As the teachers settled into their seats, another administrator and I prepared for the next 90 minutes of activities. The day's training had been organized by Joanne Kerekes, the district's respected assistant superintendent, who had been charged with ensuring teachers understood the Anti-Bullying Bill of Rights, an important new state law. The legislation, one of the most stringent laws of its type in the nation, addressed harassment, intimidation, and bullying (HIB) in schools. While many educators regarded it as important and necessary, others saw it as cumbersome and complex. Many administrators thought its labyrinthine processes set them up for failure.

Joanne knew that teachers in the district needed to learn the key facts about the HIB law *and* understand it on a more visceral, personal level. She tried to serve both purposes in her design of the training that day.

In our small group that morning, we began by showing a video that conveyed the key points of the law. I sensed the "here we go again" sentiment spreading in the room. Once the video was over, the teachers expected me to begin lecturing about the law.

Instead, once the video was over, I turned to the discussion prompts that Joanne provided us and started to share questions with the group. The conversation started slowly, but there were a couple of extroverts in the room, so I was hopeful we would have a genuine discussion. Slowly, one at a time, the teachers began to open up. They didn't just answer the questions; they allowed themselves to become very vulnerable.

One teacher talked about being marginalized and picked on in high school because of her weight. Another member of the group said he struggled academically in school for many years and felt demeaned by teachers who became frustrated with him. A third teacher, an affable athlete, talked about the guilt he still felt from being a bystander while his teammates harassed other students. By the time the session ended, nearly everyone in the room had recounted scarring experiences from decades before. A few tears were shed. It was an emotionally vulnerable session that shifted the conversation from policies and process to the law's important purpose.

Frank Warren and Brandon Stanton have both harnessed the power of the Internet and social media to provide people the opportunity to share their stories and express their vulnerability.

Warren started PostSecret in 2005 as a community art project display. Today, more than a half-million postcards with anonymous secrets have been sent to Warren's now famous Germantown, Maryland address. Every Sunday, Warren selects ten postcards to post at postsecret.com.

Some of the postcards are small handmade art projects, while others are postcards from tourist attractions. Some bear the handwriting of the author; some have computer-printed text in distinctive fonts. All of them represent the sentiments of a vulnerable author. Here are some examples:

"Every time I see a political family fall, I thank God my dad lost that race."

"I lied & said I heard voices *because I thought just being sad wasn't enough to get help.*"

Some secrets are just a short message scrawled on a black white piece of paper, like this one written in blue and red ink and adorned with purple hearts:

"Your affairs were the BEST things to ever happen to me. Now I'm with the person I've known I should be with since elementary school. I've NEVER been happier."

Another had a volleyball net, basketball, and soccer ball and drawn in marker and said,

> "I can't have a team Dinner because they will find out their coach is GAY!"

The PostSecret community has now extended to six books and a touring show based on the messages of the postcards.

Another massive social media project began with similarly humble origins. Brandon Stanton started Humans of New York as a photography project in 2010. The initial goal was to create a catalogue of the people of New York by photographing them on the street. "Somewhere along the way," Stanton writes, "I began to interview my subjects in addition to photographing them. And alongside their portraits, I'd include quotes and short stories from their lives."

The project now boasts more than 25 million followers on social media, and Stanton has captured the images and stories of people in more than 20 countries. In several special series, he's told the stories of inmates, Iraq War veterans, and the patients, parents, and staff of a cancer hospital. Stories shared with Stanton reflect the full range of human emotion, including the heartbreaking moments of life, love gained and lost, and the optimism of youth.

Warren and Stanton tap into our willingness – our eagerness even – to be vulnerable and tell our stories, given the right circumstances. Leaders understand this – like when my colleague Joanne developed the anti-bullying training. Leaders realize that students, employees and colleagues all have a compelling story.

One of my greatest privileges as a staff member at the Catholic school where I worked was serving as retreat director for the school's senior Kairos retreat. The Kairos retreat is a four-day, three-night residential retreat based on the spirituality of the St. Ignatius of Loyola, the founder of the Society of Jesus (or the Jesuits).[8] The retreat grew in popularity among Catholic – particularly Jesuit – schools in the 1980s, and it had become an integral part of St. John's by the time I started teaching there.

---

[8] The Society of Jesus is an order of Catholic priests founded in the sixteenth century by St. Ignatius. The most prominent member of the order today is Pope Francis, who was ordained a Jesuit priest in 1969.

The leadership team of each Kairos includes faculty members of the school, students, and a priest, who presides at the Masses and served as the spiritual director. Significantly, the "Rector" of the retreat was the student leader, not the priest. I first got to experience the power of Kairos as one of the teachers who gives one of the major talks during the course of the retreat.

My job as retreat director was to ensure that the retreat ran smoothly, handle student issues, and essentially serve as *in loco parentis* – albeit with the support of several other teachers – for 40 teenage boys for four days. It was a unique, joyful and scary opportunity for an educator who was still in his mid-20s. It was another significant and formative leadership experience that had a lasting impact.

What's powerful about the retreat is the intentional building of community and trust. Kairos retreats create the ideal conditions for students to be vulnerable. The student and faculty leaders set the example by sharing their stories. They're encouraged to go deep, and they do.

Separated intentionally from the roles they play back at school, the participants open up one by one, inspired by the examples of the student and staff leaders. At every Kairos retreat I attended, I was astounded at how much (to put it bluntly) "crap" the teenagers had already lived through. We heard about the impact of divorce, bullying, deaths of loved ones, and so much more. Young people desperately want to tell their stories in a safe setting, I learned, and given the right conditions they will.

The many moments of vulnerability created by the retreat had a lasting impact on the participants and the school. The Kairos retreat helped to re-humanize the school every year, and the vulnerability the seniors experienced helped them to become kinder leaders, which is especially important in an all-male school. The retreat also helped the adult participants, who experienced the vulnerability of the boys, became more sympathetic servants of them.

I carried that experience of vulnerability, years later, into my work as an assistant principal at Prior Lake High School (PLHS), a suburb of Minneapolis. In my third year in that role, I worked closely with a student on the high-functioning end of the autism spectrum who had a challenging, occasionally volatile, time getting along with his peers. I began to work with Tom when he transitioned back to our school after attending a special program for students with similar issues.

As his trust in me grew, Tom, who was bright and talkative, regularly dragged his roller bag into my office during his lunch period to work through a minor conflict with another student or just to chat. That was part of the plan we developed with Tom as he transitioned back to a regular high school. He was encouraged to see me to work through problems with his peers instead of letting them boil over.

On days when he wanted to talk, Tom wouldn't even ask permission from my secretary. He and his bag would just roll right by her. Knowing of our arrangement, she would just nod as he sped by.

One frequent topic of those conversations was NASCAR. Tom was obsessed. Driver Jeff Gordon was his favorite. Gordon, a champion racer who drove the distinctive, multi-colored #24 during much of his career, is regarded as one of the greatest in NASCAR history. After Gordon won a race, like a proud family member Tom would bring me the newspaper clipping that listed his hero as the top finisher. But if Gordon didn't do well on Sunday, the group of adults who worked with Tom were prepared for anxiety and anger on the Monday morning that followed. For the first time in my life, I found myself paying attention to NASCAR results.

One day, Tom rolled into my office, a tad more somber than usual. It was the middle of the week so I knew it wasn't about a race, but I could sense something was churning in his head.

"Hey, what's up?" I said as he stood in my doorway.

Umm. Well," he stammered a bit. Tom was usually pretty articulate so I knew something was up.

He took a couple of steps into my office, took a breath and blurted: "So-I-heard-some-kids-talking. They-said-you're-gay. Are-you?" When Tom was nervous about a topic, his speech would accelerate like Jeff Gordon's #24.

I hadn't been asked point-blank like that before. I hesitated for just a moment. I never made a big "I'm gay" announcement at the school, but my bosses, the faculty, and lots of parents and students knew. I wasn't afraid of anyone knowing. I chose to be myself.

I thought for a second about how I'd answer Tom, and said simply, "Yes. Yes, I am."

"Oh," he responded, perhaps surprised by my honesty. "People-say-Jeff-Gordon-is-gay-because-he-drives-a-rainbow-painted-car."

Thank goodness *everything* always came back to NASCAR for Tom.

"What do you think about that?" I asked.

"I guess I don't care," he said. "Okay-I-have-to-go-to-class." He turned around, bag in hand, and headed out of the office.

I wondered if Tom would continue to roll into my office after that conversation. He probably didn't know any openly gay people. If he did return, I figured it might take some time.

But he was back the next day. He continued to roll in bypassing my secretary to share whatever was on his mind. My moment of vulnerability deepened his trust in me, something that really wasn't easy for him. In subsequent conversations, Tom told me about the girls he thought were nice, and he told me about the times he got teased, which I always followed up on. I listened to him, protected him, and held him accountable when he was the one stirring the pot, which he was prone to do at times.

When I left PLHS at the end of that school year to move to New Jersey, Tom was one of the dozens of reasons it was hard to leave.

GRATITUDE

Just a few months after leaving PLHS, I was hard at work as the new principal of South Brunswick High School, looking forward to getting know the staff members of my new school.

One long-standing SBHS tradition at the beginning of every school year was an all-staff luncheon put together by volunteers. Many people contributed to the lunch by bringing a dessert or setting up the cafeteria, but the biggest job belonged to the staff members who did the cooking, no small feat for a crowd of more than 250 staff members.

During my first back-to-school luncheon as a rookie principal, my head was really spinning. It was one of the first times that the entire faculty together with me at the helm. I was trying to be friendly and remember names despite the lengthy to do list running through my head. I tried to focus on being a gracious host, however, and worked my way around the cafeteria like a groom at his wedding.

Toward the end of the lunch, Dan Caffrey, a senior member of the staff, approached me. The voice in my head said, "Uh oh." Besides being a respected math teacher in the school, Dan was a leading member of the teachers' union in the district.

"Hey, Dan. What can I do for you?"

Dan could be terse. I learned to appreciate his directness.

"Make sure you thank the cooks," he said.

"Yes, yes, of course," I stammered as he walked away. "I will. Thanks." To be honest, I had a thousand thoughts going through my head, but expressing gratitude to the people who toiled away in the kitchen wasn't one of them.

Minutes later, I took the microphone and passed on all the appropriate thank yous. Dan had saved me. It was a kind gesture that I've never forgotten. It wasn't his job to ensure that the new principal looked good. But he had taken the time to make an important point. Despite our different perspectives at times on union issues, I always appreciated Dan. And I got to be pretty good about making sure I said thank you.

Thanks to Dan and other members of the high school's staff, showing gratitude was a part of the culture of the school. For several years during my tenure as principal, for instance, we had a special initiative that encouraged teachers to write notes of appreciation to the parents of students who had made a positive impact in their classroom, extracurricular activity, or sport. We knew, of course, that parents and students would treasure the letters. I also knew from psychological studies that when someone writes and sends a letter of gratitude, there are also significant positive effects on their brains.[9]

Al Bertani, a senior consultant with the University of Chicago's Urban Education Institute, is well aware of that research – and simply knows people well. Al helped shape our practices of gratitude when I served as executive director of the Philadelphia Academy of School Leaders (Philly School Leaders). When Al

[9] See, for example, Chapter 4 of *The How of Happiness: A New Approach to Getting the Life You Want* by Sonja Lyubomirsky.

facilitated the first Summer Institute of the Neubauer Fellowship in Educational Leadership, the organization's flagship program, he made sure each guest speaker received the best kind of thank you. At the end of each session, two participants expressed their gratitude by sharing what they learned from the session. While we still gave each speaker the typical branded coffee mug or water bottle, I know that what mattered much more to them was hearing the heartfelt words shared by the principals. Everyone in the room was inspired by the sentiments expressed in those moments.

Expressing gratitude well became a signature practice of Philly School Leaders. I wrote many handwritten notes to our principals and supporters, we sent birthday cards to our Fellows, and, when thanking our benefactors, we tried to make our gifts of appreciation personal and meaningful.

The principals and my sneaky staff even turned the tables on me after our third Summer Institute. The principals had signed a soccer ball emblazoned with the logo of my favorite British soccer team, the Tottenham Hotspur. It was one of the most thoughtful gifts I had ever received.

"CLOSE TO THE CORE"

Whether I was leading a non-profit startup like Philly School Leaders or a new education policy initiative, there have been more than a few times during my leadership career when I thought to myself, "There's not enough of me to go around." I sometimes felt like I was playing an endless game of whack-a-mole. As soon as I resolved one issue, another would pop up. Damn moles.

As a principal, I got that feeling often. Sometimes it was just because of the crazy stuff that happens in a big high school like bomb threats or a group of students stealing the answer key to a big exam. Sometimes, it was just the demanding schedule. Each school year, I averaged about 100 weekend and evening activities that included concerts, sports competitions, Site Council meetings, and awards programs. It wasn't unusual for me to be at school until 8 or 9 p.m. three times a week, then turning around and starting the work day again early the next morning.

Though I love the challenge and fast pace of leadership roles, there are times when I get stretched too thin. I don't get enough sleep, and I eat poorly.

I also feel the special kind of fatigue introverts feel. I consider myself "an introvert by nature and an extrovert by training." As a principal, I enjoyed interacting with students, staff members, and parents, but I needed solitude and quiet to recharge. Finding time to do that was especially hard to do between September and June.

Even as I work hard to finish this book, I find that "there's not enough of me to go around." I work on the book eight hours a day, deal with email, work on building a new business, and try to maintain a relationship with my partner. Considering that, as I write, I've neglected my body and need to lose 25 pounds, I clearly still haven't figured it all out.

In moments like these, a voice in my head reminds me to "live close to the core."

Living close to the core, for me, means keeping a focus on those things that matter most: relationships, health, spirituality, and intellectual growth. At times when I've gotten the "there's not enough of me" feeling, I've tried to remind myself to return to what really matters. Sometimes that means returning to my foundational activities (working out and reading, for example). At other times, it means getting rid of those things in my life that inhibit my ability to thrive.

Reduce and simplify. When I began my tenure with Philly School Leaders, I started the process of selling my condominium in New Jersey where I had lived for about ten years. My partner and I did our research on staging a home for sale. We fixed some glaring issues, like the half-bath that had become a five-year painting project, and started to reduce the clutter that had accumulated for ten years. Ken and I began the process of boxing up our non-essential belongings that we wouldn't need while the condo was up for sale. To a medium-sized unit at Extra Space Storage went the golf clubs, a box of dishes from my late grandmother, five boxes of books, three boxes of baseball cards, a considerable amount of Christmas decorations and much more. While the condo looked great, with airy closets and a garage where a car could actually fit, the storage unit was literally filled to the top. It could've been used as evidence against an accused hoarder – who loves Christmas.

After several months, the condo finally sold, and we began our move to an 850-square foot apartment in Center City Philadelphia. We were excited about the change to our new urban life. We could walk to cultural events and first-rate restaurants. Not one, but two international-caliber art museums were blocks away. And, for the first time in my life since grad school in Ann Arbor, I could walk to work. But where would all of our stuff go in an apartment about half the size of the condo. And, what about that storage unit?

For about two years, it was "out of sight, out of mind." We'd occasionally visit the storage unit to retrieve some books or the Christmas decorations. Monthly, I'd grumble at the $108 charge on my credit card statement but ignore the sinking feeling that I needed to do something about it.

In the summer of 2017, I began to think seriously about a dream that I'd had for years – writing this book and being my own boss. But I knew we needed to live a bit more spartanly to make it all work. That summer I also found, in the midst of some Netflix surfing, the documentary *The Minimalists* featuring Joshua Fields Millburn and Ryan Nicodemus. "As I watched the film, I didn't just think of the storage unit brimming with junk, but all of the clutter that I had in my life that contributed nothing to my happiness. The idea of owning only 288 things like Millburn was strangely appealing.

Emboldened by Millburn, Nicodemus and a desire to get rid of a bill and stuff I didn't care about, we started to clear out the storage unit. The first phase involved going through box after box and putting things away in our apartment. Then we got rid of the more obvious things like golf clubs that were collecting cobwebs and a patio umbrella for a patio we no longer had.

Influenced by Graham Hill, founder of LifeEdited, I also started to get rid of various "keepsakes" that I had stored away. I snapped pictures of things from my childhood – a rock I painted for my mom years ago, those little plastic baseball helmets in which ice cream is served at the ballpark – then I got rid of them making a little bit more progress.

But there still wasn't an obvious home for about 250 cubic feet of stuff. So it piled up, as neatly as we could make it, in a corner of one bathroom and along the hallway by our apartment door.

Finally, I grew impatient with my overflowing drawers and the pile of boxes in our hallway. I knew I had enough gym t-shirts for about three months without doing laundry. I had novels that had gone unread through moves from Minnesota to New Jersey to Philadelphia. Enough was enough.

I issued myself a challenge: I would get rid of 500 of my possessions. Even after the cleaning out I had already accomplished, I knew I could get rid of hundreds of items, but I feared that reaching 400 or 500 would get a little painful. But that was the point, wasn't it? What did I *really* need?

So I started my personal reduction journey. I took a photo of a fake plant from IKEA and dropped it into a "500 things" folder on my phone, as I did for each object I discarded. As I progressed to item #100 (*This I Believe: The Personal Philosophies of Remarkable Men and Women*, a book of essays), I found that my objects ended up in four piles: One for the garbage, one for Goodwill, one for a used bookstore that benefits the Free Library of Philadelphia, and one – the most meaningful – for my family. As I cleaned and organized, I realized that I wanted a niece to have the afghan that my mom had crocheted and my nephew to have the Bible that bore his great-grandfather's name. I found that I got a lot of joy out of passing on those mementos, much more than I ever had in possessing them.

I found that getting rid the first 200 items (#200: a stuffed Kermit the Frog) was relatively easy. As I faced the "keep or toss" decision about an object, I repeated the words of Marie Kondo, author of *The Life-Changing Magic of Tidying Up*: "Does it spark joy?" Rarely was the answer yes.

As I reached the 300 mark (#300: a decorative Halloween candle holder), there was a bit more room in our hallway, and my drawers weren't as clogged. More stuff that we actually valued had a proper place.

Throughout the project, I was struck by the number of $15, $20, and $25 purchases I had made that easily added up to thousands of dollars. One of the worst examples was a container full of blank notebooks (I have a bit of a "Moleskin fetish"). If I saw a notebook I liked at a bookstore, I'd buy it. Then when I got home, it would get tossed into the abyss of the box, still awaiting my brilliant words.

I didn't regret all of the purchases. Kermit, after all, had been a friend for decades and an occasional prop during one of my creative lesson plans as a teacher. But clearly, the sum of those souvenir t-shirts and unread books probably amounted to a trip abroad or a fantastic weekend in New York City. But in the moment as I shopped, dopamine hit my brain and soon I was extracting the credit card from my wallet.

As I complete this chapter, I have gotten rid of nearly 400 items (#394: a golf umbrella) after about three months of simplifying. I'm also thinking about the other things that clutter my life like podcast episodes, iPhone apps, and my unresolved propensity to buy books I will never have the time to read. Though our two cats, Hugo and Gaston, look at me suspiciously when I talk about the next steps toward a more minimalist life, I'm excited about the journey.

Equilibrium and reset. After I served as a principal for eight years, I decided to pursue my interest in education policy as a senior leader of the New Jersey Department of Education (NJDOE). In my final year at the NJDOE, I had a fascinating and challenging job. I was appointed to oversee the 14 state-operated and state-monitored school districts, which fed my growing desire to work closely with urban districts. It wasn't unusual for me to crisscross the state for multiple meetings in a given day. I was constantly in the car, stopping far too often at the New Jersey's finest Dunkin' Donuts. After a few months in the role, however, a part of me began to insist, "You're not taking care of yourself. There's not enough of you to go around" and "You're a bit off track. You've got to live closer to the core."

I clearly wasn't looking after myself in the midst of a stressful, challenging job. At one point, the lowest disc in my back revolted, forcing me to listen to the wise counsel of the voice in my head. I woke up one morning, and when I tried to walk I almost passed out from the pain. When I moved, it felt like someone was shooting an electric shock down my lower back and left leg. I remember lying on my couch, leg propped up, waiting to get an appointment with a back specialist, as a superintendent griped to me about a state employee she detested. I had to make some changes in my life.

Once I was somewhat mobile again, I started making some changes. I started to take long walks, sometimes twice a day, and my diet improved. I essentially hit the "reset" button in order to recover a sense of equilibrium.

In those moments when my life is off-kilter, like when I was laid out with back pain, I know I have to hit "reset." The reset process for me begins with insistent voice in my head, asking, "What's the most important thing you do every day?" The answer – besides telling my partner I love him – is getting some physical activity or going to the gym. Working out is the keystone to my mental and physical health. When the keystone is out of place, the structure of my life is precarious.

When I'm at my best, I think about my life being in equilibrium: There's just the right blend of friends and family, time for just Ken and me, work that matters, physical activity, intellectual stimulation, and solitude or, as I call it, "Tim time." In order for me to thrive, I need to live by that formula.

Flow. I started the conceptual work on this book while still serving as Executive Director of Philly School Leaders. Before heading to work, I'd try to spend an hour before work several times a week working through my ideas about leadership that lasts. As I read, brainstormed, and jotted down notes, the hour would feel like five or ten minutes. I'd get immersed in working through a concept, and I'd lose track of time. I'd feel deeply contented and satisfied by the "work."

Mihaly Csíkszentmihályi would not be surprised. The psychologist and researcher termed this feeling "flow." During flow, Csíkszentmihályi suggests, we're totally engaged in what we're doing. We're absorbed and fulfilled. Time flies by as we get lost in the moment.

I've felt a state of flow a number of times when writing this book. I'd look up from my MacBook after working on a few pages and realize that I was pretty hungry and *really* had to pee. Then I'd look at the clock on my laptop and realize three hours had flown by.

When my life is in equilibrium – when I'm taking care of mind, body, spirit – I know that I experience more moments of flow. I experience the quick passing of an evening with Ken and good friends. I feel the sun on my shoulders and sweat dripping from my body as I jog on a warm summer day.

I remember a particular instance of equilibrium and flow during my days as a principal. The school had just concluded another successful pep rally. A number of students had been recognized for achievements in academics, athletics, and service. As underclass students headed to catch their buses, Student Council members had animated conversations about the best moments of the rally as they cleaned up the gym. In one corner, a few teachers decked out in school colors congratulated some of the students who had just been honored. Lots of seniors were just hanging out in no particular hurry to leave. There were kids of every hue represented: White, African-American, South Asian, Latin. Gay and straight. Our DJ for the rally continued to spin songs. Even he didn't want to leave. The kids laughed, flirted, a few started dancing. They looked as profoundly happy as I felt.

CHAPTER SEVEN

DISCOVER

"Timoteo, no sabes lo que haciendo," a sassy ten-year-old Dominican girl said as she squeezed soapy water out of a pair of her brother's pants.

I smirked at her, as I tried to get the dirt out of one of my work shirts. *"La verdad. No sé nada. ¿Que estoy haciendo mal?"* It's true. I don't know what I'm doing. What am I doing wrong?

I was a highly-educated American teacher but I simply couldn't produce the magical *squish* sound that indicated that I was actually getting my clothes clean.

It was July 1992. I was trying to wash my clothes by hand amid the very clear *squishes* of the five women and girls gathered in the small courtyard of a house in Las Matas de Farfan, Dominican Republic (DR), a town about 20 miles east of the Haitian border. Overhead lines that crisscrossed the courtyard were already hung with clean, wet clothes.

Washing clothes was "always a humbling experience," I noted in my journal that summer. I had come to the DR as a leader of high school students on a service trip, but often found myself being taught by the very people I was supposed to be serving.

As I tried diligently to produce that magical *squish*, Nini, the mother of the family who had opened their home to me, lovingly smiled and shook her head at my lack of clothes-washing skills, an expression I got used to during the month I spent with her family. I adored Nini.

Rosamilia, the ten-year-old, tried to correct my methods to little or no effect. I finished washing my pile of clothes. They were clean enough for me.

"Bastante. Terminado. ¡No mas!" I told them as my "clean" clothes lie in a bucket ready to dry in the 90-degree air. Enough. I'm finished.

I was the only male in the midst of the clothes washing. That task, in this Dominican town, was something that only women and girls did. While Rosamilia had offered to do my wash, I insisted that I do it myself. Though it wasn't my place to condemn the gender roles of the family who graciously hosted me, I didn't need to perpetuate them either. I wanted to respect their culture and share a bit of mine, and that meant gender didn't matter when it came to tackling dirty clothes.

It was bad enough that Nini wouldn't sit down at the family table for the big meal of the day when the father of the family, Marcelo, and I came home for dinner around noon. Decades later, my mouth still waters when I think of the meals Nini and her daughters would put down on the dinner table in the shade at the edge of the courtyard: dishes heaping with chicken, rice, beans, and – my favorite – plantains.

I would arrive at my Dominican home for dinner after keeping an eye on the work of the high school students who were on the service trip. We'd spend the morning painting a church, digging the foundation for a house, or helping out at an orphanage, then head to our respective hosts' homes for dinner.

"El Señor" and I usually ate silently, with an occasional "Buen provecho!" to show our approval of Nini's cooking. Marcelo was thoroughly Dominican, speaking rapidly while frequently dropping the "s" off plurals. Though my comprehension of Spanish was good enough to communicate with the rest of the family, it was hard to hold a conversation with him.

After *El Señor* finished his meal and headed to his room for a little siesta, I usually lingered a bit, and Nini would sit down and eat with me. It was another little symbolic rebellion at Dominican gender roles. Nini would speak slowly for me, and I'd tell her about my morning in broken Spanish. I really valued that time.

Nini was slightly less limited by the mores of Dominican culture. Yes, she led the cooking and the cleaning, but she also contributed a little money to the family. Nini made a few pesos here and there doing neighbor ladies' hair in a shack the family had converted into a little beauty shop. With Nini's small contributions and savings from Marcelo's salary as the *director* or principal of the local elementary school, the family had put together enough money to buy a dump truck that their 19-year-old son drove for construction jobs. They were better off than most families in Las Matas.

As I wrapped up my own laundry that hot July day, the ladies chattered away. (Gossip is universal.) I retrieved a t-shirt from my bucket of clean clothes, wrung it out one final time, then reached for the nearest low-hanging overhead line.

"*NOOOOOOO, Timoteo,*" one of the ladies screeched. She pointed at the line I was approaching with wet laundry, and shouted, "*¡Para electricidad!*" That's for electricity!

Startled, I dropped the shirt on the dusty ground as the other ladies laughed. Yet another learning experience in the DR. The *americano* had to be watched or else he'd electrocute himself.

I laughed along with them in the moment, but I was also embarrassed. I could've hurt myself or one of them. I was humbled yet again. It wasn't the first or the last time that summer as Rosamilia corrected my Spanish or when a local twelve-year-old taught me how to correctly mix cement. I wanted to learn about Dominican culture – to explore their world – and washing my clothes their way had taught me a lot.

As my shirts and pants dried on the correct clothesline that night, I wrote in my journal, "At least I provided the neighbor ladies with a good laugh." Silly gringo.

From moments like that day trying to wash clothes in the DR to many other significant learning experiences in my life, I've noted three key elements to the process of discovery: Humility, curiosity, and information-seeking. Let's explore each in detail.

HUMILITY

> When pride comes, then comes disgrace,
> but with humility comes wisdom.
> Proverbs 11:2

Inextricably linked to the process of discovery is humility. Curious people are typically quite humble about how little they know. As David Brooks writes in *Road to Character,* "Humility is the awareness that there's a lot you don't know and that a lot of what you think you know is distorted or wrong." Humility, he continues, is "the moral quality of knowing what you don't know and figuring out a way to handle your ignorance, uncertainty, and limitation." The best leaders handle their ignorance by being open to growth.

Humility, as I learned throughout the summer I spent in the DR, and the process of discovery interact powerfully. The process of discovery, like the afternoon spent washing clothes, humbled me, and that humility expanded my openness to absorbing everything around me. That curiosity spurred further discovery. It became essentially a cycle that reinforced itself:

$$\text{Discovery} \Rightarrow \text{Humility} \Rightarrow \text{Openness and Curiosity} \Rightarrow$$
$$\text{Discovery} \Rightarrow \text{and so forth}$$

When our lives are characterized by humility and a discovery mindset, we're continually reminded of how much we have to learn. But that doesn't discourage us. It just makes us more eager. We want to jump in and take risks. Because we know and accept the limitations of our knowledge, we're willing to look a little foolish along the way. We're eager to know more about ourselves and our world.

In Jim Collins' classic business study, *Good to Great*, he was surprised to find that the best CEOs are more likely to be modest work horses than charismatic hard-chargers. Collins and his research team found that executives who led their companies from "good to great" possessed "extreme personal humility with intense professional will." These so-called Level 5 leaders[10] "never wanted to become larger-than-life heroes," the study found. "They never aspired to be put on a pedestal or become unreachable icons. They were seemingly ordinary people quietly producing extraordinary results." Level 5 leaders set aside their egos to focus their ambitions on the organization, not themselves.

Interestingly, these leaders were also more likely than their less successful peers to attribute their success to factors outside of themselves. They were more likely to attribute results to luck or the hard work of their employees than to their own efforts.

---

[10] Level 5 "refers to a five-level hierarchy of executive capabilities, with Level 5 at the top," Collins writes.

Conversely, when things went poorly for their company, they were more likely to assign responsibility to themselves.

In their understated way, these top leaders communicated their humility, perhaps unknowingly, and their colleagues noticed. "Those who worked with or wrote about good-to-great leaders continually used words like quiet, humble, modest, reserved, shy, gracious, mild-mannered, self-effacing, understated. . . .and so forth," Collins explains.

I suggest that the success of these leaders isn't just because they possessed both humility and will, but that that former enhanced the impact of the latter. Their modesty about their capacities may have ensured that they were more open to the expertise of others, much as I described in the cycle above. Because of their humility, they sought out more data and advice. Then, when they exercised their professional will, they could do so in a smarter way than those CEOs who approached their role more egotistically.

Across my career, I've visited hundreds of schools. I often look at principal leadership during those visits through the lens of Level 5 leadership. I try to take note of patterns in the principal's language. I get skeptical very quickly when I hear principals use a lot of first-person language:

"I raised student achievement by 10 points last year."

"I reduced the number of discipline incidents by 15%."

Instead, I know from personal experience that achieving anything great in an organization as complex as a school is about "we," not "I." I know I'm in the presence of a great principal when I hear,

"Our students and teachers worked hard and got our test scores up 10 points last year."

"We reduced discipline incidents by 15%. It's all because our teachers set high expectations in their classrooms, and our students met them."

Gains made when the principal is emphasizing "I" over "we" are not sustainable. Teachers, who most surely contributed to the positive trends, will feel disenfranchised. We all know it's hard to follow an egotistical leader who takes credit for organizational achievements. We'd rather work for a Level 5 leader.

Discovery begins with the admission that you don't know and can't do everything. You're constantly seeking new and better answers. You're willing to put yourself in the hands of a teacher or mentor, and you respect the expertise of others.

Many widely-admired business leaders model this humble, discovery mindset. According to the entrepreneurship education firm Empact, some of the most successful live by the "five-hour rule." Bill Gates, Warren Buffett, Oprah Winfrey, for example, dedicate at least five hours each week to reading or other forms of discovery. Arthur Blank, the co-founder of Home Depot and owner of the Atlanta Falcons, reads at least two hours a day. Gates is a particularly voracious reader who often shares his recommendations.[11] In the more than two years I worked closely with philanthropist Joe Neubauer, I found that he had one of the most curious intellects of anyone I've known. It was undoubtedly integral to his success. Clearly, the accomplishments of these leaders didn't diminish their eagerness to know more. Those who are humble are able to discover and, through open-minded discovery, they are humbled.

CURIOSITY

Humility, as I noted above, is inextricably connected to curiosity and discovery – even for the business leaders we just discussed. Humility is what fosters a mind open to discovery, and curiosity is what drives it. My own curiosity has served me well throughout my career – from teaching to leading a school to developing the talents of other leaders.

Curiosity and teaching. Curiosity is an essential part of being a great teacher. The best teachers are themselves eager learners. They're reading the last scientific studies, reading the latest novel, or consuming hours of CNN.

Curiosity served me well as a teacher. I rarely repeated the same exact lesson. I was always tweaking as I learned more, especially for my American Government class. It wasn't unusual

---

[11] www.gatesnotes.com/Books#All

for me to get material for a lesson from NPR during my drive to school.

A teacher's eagerness to know more about the content they teach – like computer science or fourth grade language arts – isn't the only way curiosity shapes effective teaching. Great teachers also have a deep interest in understanding how each of their students learn. This form of curiosity enables teachers to pick up on the subtlest of signals. They're attuned to students' mood changes. They know that a visual representation of a concept will help one student learn, while a telling anecdote will click with another. They know which students to push, which to encourage, and which to leave alone.

For forty years, Lou Volpe taught at Harry Truman High School in working-class Levittown, Pennsylvania, about 25 miles from Center City Philadelphia. He used his keen insight and willingness to push the boundaries of high school theater to impact the lives of two generations of teenagers. His career and Truman's exemplary theater program are profiled in Michael Sokolove's book, *Drama High: The Incredible True Story of a Brilliant Teacher, a Struggling Town, and the Magic of Theater*. The NBC series *Rise* is inspired by *Drama High* and Lou Volpe.

Volpe, as we learn in *Drama High*, is very intuitive in directing his student actors. His curiosity about each of his students strengthens his teaching. By truly understanding them, he can draw out their best performances. It's the opposite of the "one size fits all" approach of many classrooms.

Volpe talks about directing two boys, Bobby and Zach, who are best friends and co-leads in one of his productions. They require very different approaches as a director and teacher. Bobby thinks like an actor; Zach does not. "I see [Bobby's] mind turning in every conversation we have. He takes everything in that I'm saying – he listens, he really does – but he has his own thoughts and his own insights," Volpe explains.

In contrast, the teacher has to draw on Zach's "dynamic sense of commitment" – he's a "bulldog" in Volpe's words – to draw out a strong performance. In the end, he's successful in hitting just the right notes in directing both. Along with their castmates, Bobby and Zach earn a standing ovation at the prestigious International Thespian Festival, the Super Bowl of high school theater.

Volpe and other great teachers aren't just eager to create the "light bulb moments" talked about by many teachers. Volpe, I suggest, was more interested in "light switches." Great teachers know not only how to get students to understand them (the light bulb moment), but how to get them to internalize and synthesize knowledge. The bulb lights up brighter when many connections in a student's mind are made between new knowledge, their previous learning, and their own reality. Volpe found the switch in the young actor Bobby so that he listened to his director *and* generated his own insights. What results is a powerful form of learning that isn't quickly forgotten.

Curiosity and leading. Effective leaders are similarly attuned to the people in their organization. They are curious about the "light switches" that activate their team members' motivations. They take the time necessary to listen and understand.

As a brand-new principal, I was eager to listen to and understand what the school's key stakeholders thought about the school. I was curious about what priorities students, parents, staff members would identify for the new principal. I invited everyone to make an appointment to meet with me individually or in small groups. In those conversations I posed three simple questions:

- What's working well here?
- What's not working well?
- Is there anything else you want me to know?

Those three simple questions generated pages and pages of helpful advice about how to approach leadership of the school.

By the time I finished the discussions, I had talked to close to 150 members of the school community, including dozens of parents who showed up for my first School Site Council meeting that September.

From those conversations, I discovered a lot. I identified some very clear themes that required long-term attention and a few "low-hanging fruit" that I could address immediately. Though time-consuming, these meetings were one of the smartest things I did as a principal.

Throughout my tenure as a principal at South Brunswick High School my boss was the widely-respected Superintendent Gary McCartney. During our eight years working together we collaborated well, and I learned a great deal from Gary. To this day, when faced with a complex challenge, I hear Gary's voice in my head: "Knowledge is power."

Gary is an excellent role model for curiosity as a leader. Before every contentious School Board Meeting or parent conference, he wanted to be fully knowledgeable of the issue at hand. He wanted to understand the people involved – their needs and motivations. He was unfailingly well-prepared, driven by a deep-seated curiosity about every issue he confronted.

I tried to follow his example in leading the high school. When dealing with the most serious discipline issues in the school, for example, I would work with the assistant principals to conduct a thorough investigation before I talked to the "alleged perpetrators." I wanted to know as many of the facts before I questioned them. Once I sat down with them I'd begin posing questions. If I felt they were lying or holding back on information, I'd say to them, "You know. I don't ask questions that I don't already know the answer to. Do you want to try to answer that question again?" By letting my curiosity lead the way in these investigations, I was better equipped to get to the bottom of them. Knowledge is power.

Curiosity, developing leaders, and empathic listening. After serving as a principal and state education official, I had the great privilege of serving as the first Executive Director of the Philadelphia Academy of School Leaders. In that role, I had the good fortune to get to know many amazing educators in the city, several of whom enlisted me as a mentor.

In mentoring the principals and other leaders in my career, I've always tried my best, as Stephen Covey urged, to "seek first to understand, then to be understood." This notion, the fifth of *The Seven Habits of Highly Effective People*, argues that we need to be curious at a much deeper level when we communicate. Covey wrote,

> "We typically seek first to be understood. Most people do not listen with intent to understand; they listen with the intent to reply. They're either speaking or preparing to speak. They're filtering everything through their own paradigms, reading their autobiography into other people's lives."

I like to believe that, most of the time, I avoid these kinds of errors. When I worked in schools, for example, I found that my ability to listen helped me build rapport quickly with students and parents. My curiosity about what makes people tick served me well.

I like to believe I listen with empathy. In working with Philadelphia principals, I found that when the principals shared a problem or frustration with me, I listened intently. I truly wanted to understand the problem and be helpful. But my room for growth was in my tendency to jump in quickly and start to frame potential ways to address the problem. I might be a great problem-solver, but Covey would not have found me to be an empathic listener.

Empathic listening, Covey wrote, requires us to set aside our egos and get "inside another person's frame of reference. You look out through it, you see the world the way they see the world, you understand their paradigm, you understand how they feel." Empathic listening reflects a deep curiosity not only with what the other person is saying, but how they're experiencing what they're talking about. I would have been a better mentor if I had worked harder to see the problem from the principal's perspective and became more attuned to her emotions about it. Then, and only then, should I work in collaboration with the principal to problem-solve together, beginning with what's on her mind and potential options.

Stalls, jerks, and bumps. Whether I was teaching, leading or mentoring, I was always mindful that moments of curiosity and discovery can be laden with frustration and even exasperation. I've learned, however, that the bumps we encounter as we learn and explore can lead to some unintended new understandings that can be applied to other aspects of our lives.

This was definitely the case as I learned to drive a manual transmission when I was in my 30s. My capable mentor in this endeavor was my boyfriend at the time. Steve needed our larger, more reliable vehicle for a work assignment, so I would need to start driving his five-speed Eagle Summit.

I had first tried to learn how to drive a stick-shift as a 16-year-old in my family's new Honda Civic. I was not a very mechanical kid so I was anxious at the outset. Before we left our driveway, my gentle, kind father ran through the basics – how to drive with two feet, how to release smoothly on the clutch, how to shift from first gear to second, and so forth.

"Got it?" he asked. I nodded. "OK, push down on the clutch and let the car glide down the driveway into the street. Then let's give it a go."

I executed the glide successfully, then placed my foot on the clutch, put the care in first gear, and started to release pressure – too quickly – only to feel car jerk violently and hear the tires squeal until I hit the brakes.

My dad gritted his teeth and reiterated the lesson about the clutch. I put my feet in the proper places again and started to release the clutch.

Jerk! Squeal! Again.

I could see pained expression on my dad's face. My father treated his cars like pets. They *were* his pets. I felt awful.

The process continued for what seemed like an hour, but it was probably about five minutes. Lesson. Jerk. Squeal. Exasperation. Lesson. Jerk. Squeal. Exasperation.

We both got frustrated. His impatience grew painfully obvious.

A few blocks from our house, he said tersely, "That's enough for today."

"Fine," I said, got out of the driver's seat, and let him drive home.

Through unsaid mutual agreement, we never tried it again. Learning the skill wasn't a necessity. I had my own car with an automatic transmission. I never got the skill down.

My boyfriend Steve, fortunately, was more patient – probably because he didn't care as much about the Eagle Summit. I was also better prepared to be patient with myself. Older and more confident, I was mentally prepared for the jerks and bumps. I was a high school assistant principal after all. I can do this.

After a verbal refresher course from Steve, I managed to get from first gear to third in a vacant parking lot. Yes, there were occasional jerks and one or two tire squeals, but it was obvious I was getting the hang of it. After several practice sessions, Steve released me to the streets of St. Louis Park, Minnesota. Slowly but surely, I made progress.

As I learned to drive the five-speed and experienced the feeling of being a novice again, I couldn't help but think of many of the students I had gotten to know as an assistant principal. For most of the students I worked with, school wasn't a place where they felt successful. Because of learning disabilities, mental health problems, or problems at home, their process of discovery at school was difficult, much harder than learning to drive a manual transmission. Some of them dreaded school as much I disliked the thought of getting back into the driver's seat of the Honda Civic as a 16-year-old.

I shared a few stories of my "driver's education" at school. One student I worked with, an outdoorsy kid who liked to work on cars, had a particularly good laugh at my expense, and I was fine with that. I also shared what I learned in a brief item in the faculty newsletter. "For many of our students," I wrote, "learning is full of the stalls, jerks, and bumps that you would experience riding with me in a car with a manual transmission." Revisiting the path of discovery, I explained, reminds us how it feels to learn.

SEEKING INFORMATION AND IDEAS

"Good ideas come from everywhere.
It's more important to recognize a good idea than to author it."
– attributed to Jeanne Gang, architect and McArthur Fellow

Whether we want to learn how to drive a manual transmission or explore a much more substantial topic, we are well-served by humility and a driving curiosity. To satisfy that curiosity, we need to take the next important step. We need to seek out information and ideas.

From the creation of the scientific method to other disciplined forms of exploration, we have found that discovery and the process of seeking out new ideas and information greatly benefit from structure and direction.

Two approaches of particular interest to education and social science provide shape and form for the process of gathering information and ideas. Rooted in a discovery mindset, design theory and improvement science both seek to solve problems and meet needs.

Design thinking. Design thinking utilizes creative strategies to address complex problems and create solutions for them. This methodology is now employed not just in the creative arts like architecture or industrial design, but increasingly in business and education.

Stanford's Hasso Plattner Institute of Design (the "d.school") identifies five key modes for the approach: empathize, define, ideate, prototype, and test.

Of particular interest to our discussion of discovery is the "empathize" phase. During this stage, the people involved in a design project focus on the human aspects of the challenge. As the d.school puts it, the empathize stage involves "your effort to understand the way [the clients] do things and why, their physical and emotional needs, how they think about world, and what is meaningful to them." During this stage, participants might adopt an ethnographic approach and conduct observations or interviews. Through close contextual study, the team is able to design better solutions.

Great designers place great emphasis on the human side of their work. Raymond Loewy created the looks of the Exxon logo, Coca-Cola vending machines, and even Air Force One. Loewy was in the words of the *Harvard Business Review*, an "anthropologist first, an artist second." Architect and MacArthur genius grant recipient Jeanne Gang believes she's a "relationship-builder" first and foremost. "Most people think architects design buildings and cities, but what we really design are relationships," she explains.

Design thinking can be a useful lens for leaders seeking innovative solutions to the challenges they experience. As they seek those solutions, leaders will also develop a more complete understanding of the experiences of people in their organizations.

Improvement science. With roots in the health care industry's efforts to improve hospital outcomes, improvement science seeks to help organizations get better at getting better. It's a multidisciplinary approach that an increasing number of organizations, including schools and school districts, now use to enhance their ability to get better at core functions. Improvement science places an emphasis on testing potential solutions and spreading them through networks of organizations in a particular field. Approaches that are found to actually work can then be disseminated and used elsewhere.

The Carnegie Foundation for Teaching is the leading proponent of applying improvement science to educational settings. The Foundation identifies six core principles for the approach, the first of which is most relevant to this discussion: "Make the work problem-centered and user-focused."

This step requires careful collection of data about the experiences of those involved in the issue. For an exploration of chronic student absenteeism, for example, a principal might pose these questions: What do students say are the most common reasons for missing school? Are there particular days of the week or months of the year when they miss the most school? What do parents say about their children's absences?

Though they attack problems and needs of individuals and organizations somewhat differently, design thinking and improvement science both begin their disciplined approaches to information-seeking with an emphasis on the human experience.

The first "O." The military strategist John Boyd was also very interested in how people gathered and processed information and made decisions. An eclectic thinker with an illustrious career, Boyd's work drew from sources as diverse as chaos theory, the second law of thermodynamics, and quantum mechanics. He was, interestingly, an influential air-to-air combat strategist, but had no combat kills himself. Vice President Dick Cheney was a fan and consulted with him on the plans for Operation Desert Storm. The design of the U.S. Air Force fighter planes still reflects Boyd's influence two decades after his death. Today he's is regarded as the most influential military strategist who hardly anyone knows about. As journalist James Fallows wrote upon his death in 1997, "His ideas about weapons, leadership, and the very purpose of national security changed the modern military."

One of Boyd's most significant contributions to strategic thinking is the "OODA loop," which is now applied to a variety of settings, including sports and business. OODA stands for Observe, Orient, Decide, and Act. Though typically framed as a set of linear stages – that's where the "loop" comes in – it's better described as a complex decision-making system.

The OODA loop attempts to capture decision-making in an ambiguous, uncertain, rapidly changing environment. Boyd identified three aspects of the "observe" part of the system:

unfolding circumstances, outside information, and unfolding interaction with the environment.

In a professional football game, for example, a quarterback is quickly taking in lots of data as he prepares for a play:

- *Unfolding circumstances:* As he heads back to the huddle, he notices a defensive back limping slightly.
- *Outside information:* His offensive coordinator relays a play through the earpiece in his helmet.
- *Unfolding interaction with the environment:* The quarterback feels his fingers stiffen just a bit as the wind kicks up and the chill factor dips below freezing.

The quarterback needs to process all of this information almost simultaneously. That's part of the "orient" part of the model. Boyd considered how the information that's gathered gets processed. The processing is influenced by characteristics of the observer including culture, experiences, and the ability to synthesize the information.

To extend the football example, the quarterback's processing of the information could be influenced by these questions: Does the team's culture encourage or discourage audibles[12]? Does the quarterback feel positive about his experiences with the offensive coordinator's play-calling? Does the quarterback resemble Tom Brady or Eeyore in the speed and effectiveness of his information-processing?

Fundamentally, the objective is to go through the OODA loop faster and smarter than your competitors. Then you'll achieve more success. When employed successfully, Fallows explains, OODA means "anticipating the other side's most likely next move, and responding in a way that counters it, faster than the opponent can adjust."

School leaders may find this framework useful in a variety of situations. A new principal, for example, might inherit a toxic climate and need to assess the environment and work quickly to effect change. Another administrator might utilize the OODA loop when required state assessments change as they often do. The loop could be effective in helping a principal make the best decisions about preparing students for the new test as she sorts

---

[12] When a team on offense is ready to run a play, a quarterback can "call an audible" and change the play if he believes the alternative will be more successful.

through all of the information flowing from state education officials, teachers, parents, and other stakeholders.

MBWA. While the OODA loop might be a new concept to some leaders, an approach more familiar to school principals and other leaders on the front lines of organizations is known by the abbreviation MBWA: management by wandering around.

MBWA has its roots in contingency models of leadership. Influenced by Frederick W. Taylor's scientific theory of management and the famous Hawthorne studies of the 1920s, contingency theorists see leadership occurring in a complex system of leader traits and internal and external factors like technology, collective bargaining, government regulation, and competition. Contingency models presume that there's no single *right* way to lead. The correct approach is shaped by the particular characteristics of the leader and the situation. In contingency models, the best leaders

- Are curious about their environment – inside and outside of the organization – and constantly process data about it.
- Understand their leadership skills and those of their colleagues.
- Are able to match leadership capabilities and approaches with the organization's needs as shaped by its environment.

Management experts Paul Hersey and Ken Blanchard further extended the contingency models as they developed situational leadership theory in the 1970s. Also a dynamic model, the situational leadership approach is task-relevant. The most effective leaders are those who adapt their leadership style to the abilities and willingness of the individual or group they are attempting to lead or influence. The situational perspective, thus, puts an emphasis on a myriad of variables that impact the effectiveness of the leader. These include the characteristics of the leader as well as the group being influenced, and the details of the task, job or function that needs to be performed.

Situational leadership theory resonates with me not only from my experiences, but from reading the research on principals' impact on student academic achievement. Principals have many important responsibilities, but across all of their key responsibilities the one with the greatest correlation to their student's academic performance is not what most people would expect. It's not school discipline or knowledge of curriculum. It's *situational awareness*. Robert Marzano, who has spent his career reviewing essentially all of the quantitative research on K-12 education, identifies situational awareness as having the largest effect size on student's learning. [13]

As a principal, I frequently sought to enhance my situational awareness by managing while wandering around. My walks around school, besides affording me some exercise and a few minutes out of the office, allowed me to take a quick environmental scan of the building. After being in high schools for so many years, I consciously and subconsciously picked up important data using this approach.

It was always critical those scans occur unpredictably. As I wandered, I was able to listen to productive and unproductive noise from classrooms. I could pick up on those rooms where students were completely absorbed in discussions, lab experiments, and making beautiful music. I also noted those rooms where movies were the prevalent "instruction," and others where only the teacher talked.

Sometimes on my MBWA excursions, I'd pick up on little things here and there, and I'd tip off an assistant principal. I might tell her, "There's a lot of energy in the air this afternoon. Let's get a few extra adults outside while the buses are loading." At other times, my thorough environmental scan of the building might lead me to the smell of chocolate chip cookies baking in a culinary class that would require further investigation.

Questioning. Colleagues, friends, and family members all tell me that one of my most "endearing" traits is my frequent use of the phrase, "I'm skeptical." It's true, though. I *am* prone to question. A lot of things. At the gym, I question "bro science," the word-of-mouth "knowledge" passed on among the guys in sleeveless t-shirts. I question all treatments for the common cold

---

[13] It's important to note the differences among the most important responsibilities are small, but situational awareness is at the top of the list with a .33 correlation to student academic achievement according to Marzano, Waters, and McNulty's *School Leadership that Works*.

except rest and time. I also question whether my cats actually like me – or just like the fact that they can coerce me into feeding them.

I've found, however, that my skeptical, questioning nature has served me well as a leader. Questioning, research clearly tells us, is essential to leadership, innovation, and organizational success.

In *The Innovator's DNA: Mastering the Five Skills of Disruptive Innovators*, Jeffrey Dyer, Hal Gregersen, and Clayton Christensen describe the findings of their six-year study of what distinguishes entrepreneurial CEOs like Herb Kelleher of Southwest Airlines and Jeff Bezos of Amazon. They found that these innovative CEOs spent 50% more time on five "discovery activities" – Associating, questioning, observing, experimenting and networking. They called those skills "the innovator's DNA."

Innovators, they found, "have a passion for inquiry." The innovative leaders they studied pose questions "to better understand what is and what might be. They ignore safe questions and opt for more crazy ones, challenging the status quo and often threatening the powers that be with uncommon intensity and frequency." Innovators like Steve Jobs "ask questions to understand how things really are today, why they are that way, and how they might be changed or disrupted. Collectively, their questions provoke new insights, connections, possibilities, and directions."

Hal Gregersen further refined this line of inquiry and developed the "catalytic questioning" technique. This process begins with identifying a problem that a team cares about intellectually and emotionally – "engaging head and heart" in other words. The team then sets out to generate at least 50 or more questions about the problem. The process doesn't allow for introductions to the questions or any attempts at answering them. Questions and only questions are allowed with time to pause between them for the team to think, reflect, and generate more questions. Even when the group struggles to generate more questions, push on, advises Gregersen. Once the team has generated enough questions, the members identify three or four questions that "seem most 'catalytic,' or which ones hold the most potential for disrupting the status quo." Finally, the team knows the best questions to explore.

Questioning was a hallmark trait of the Brazilian company Semco Partners under the leadership of maverick CEO Ricardo

Semler. At Semco, Semler led a company based on a radical form of corporate democracy. As he wrote in his book *The Seven-Day Weekend: Changing the Way Work Works*, "Ask why. Ask it all the time, ask it any day, every day, and always ask it three times in a row." This "why"-focused culture of question

> "means putting aside all the rote or pat answers that have result from what I call 'calcified' thinking, that state of mind where ideas have become so hardened that they're no longer of any use. Employees must be free to question, to analyze, to investigate; and a company must be flexible enough to listen to the answers."

Taiichi Ohno, the father of the Toyota Production System, proposed an interactive process that went even farther than Semler: "Ask 'why' five times about every matter." Pose a "why" question, answer it, and then pose another "why" based on the response. Only after the fifth "Why" question, do we get to the most important response – the root cause. "The root cause of any problem is the key to a lasting solution," Ohno said.

Richard DuFour, the distinguished school administrator and author of a number of books on leadership and learning, valued the process of questioning as well. DuFour insisted that educators keep three essential questions in mind:

- What do we want each student to learn?
- How will we know when each student has learned it?
- How will we respond when a student experiences difficulty in learning?

I referred to these questions frequently as an assistant principal and principal. A school's ability to answer the questions positively and honestly is a strong indicator of its quality.

These questions can easily be modified for any organization that claims to be knowledge-based. They might be rephrased to say,

- What do our team members need to know?
- How do we determine whether or not that they know it?
- What will we do if they don't know what we need them to know?

These questions could work for a company, military unit, or sports team. If an organization can ensure that team members *really* know what they need to know, then they are well on their way to success.

I visited DuFour's Stevenson High School in Lincolnshire, Illinois three times during his leadership of the school. There's no doubt that the school had a discovery mindset and, to use business author James Kerr's term, an "interrogative culture."

I admired Stevenson's focus on inquiry, and as principal, I tried to reinforce my own school's interrogative culture in a number of ways. For instance, when one of our assistant principals came to me to consult on a student or faculty issue, I posed these questions:

- Is there any essential background information I need to understand about this issue?
- What happened today? (Followed by some clarifying questions)
- What do you think we need to do?

Because I believed we had administrators with good judgment, more often than not, I'd channel my inner Jean-Luc Picard[14] and say, "Make it so."

At times, though, my questions helped to cause some reflection. Sometimes the administrator would say, "Let's gather some more information" or "I think I need to come up with more options." The re-thinking prompted by questioning usually resulted in better decisions.

I also wanted students to value questioning. I tried to signal this by regularly putting myself – and assistant principals at times – in front of the Student Senate to answer their questions. It was like a kinder version of "Question Time," the weekly interrogation of the Prime Minister in parliamentary systems.

The Senators' questions weren't filtered; they asked what was on their mind. Their questions could be tough at times, particularly during the budget cuts caused by the Great Recession, but the students were always respectful. The presence of administrators at these meetings sent a message, especially in a large high school, that we saw the value of standing before our students and responding to whatever was on their minds.

---

[14] See *Star Trek: The Next Generation.* He happens to be my favorite captain of the Enterprise.

MORE AND BETTER

The assistant principals and I put ourselves in front of the Student Senate because we valued students' opinions and sincerely believed they could help us improve the school. Great leaders value those interactions. They are fiercely driven by their discovery orientation to improve and master themselves and their work. Their efforts begin with the humility that they're imperfect and have much to learn. They are curious about their organization, and they want to understand themselves as leaders more fully. They seek out answers to their questions and gather relevant information so that they can make the best decisions. Their humility, curiosity, and learning are inextricably linked with their drive for knowing *more* and doing *better*.

Having spent ten years as a student and staff member at St. John's Jesuit High School in Toledo, my leadership has undoubtedly been shaped by the principles of the Jesuits. I've been particularly influenced by the Ignatian notion of *magis* – or "more" – drawn from the Jesuit motto *ad majorem Dei Gloriam* ("to the greater glory of God"). In the setting of a Jesuit school, obviously the term carries a specific Christian connotation. To me as a leader of secular organizations, the meaning of *magis* has focused on the words more, better, and greater. What *more* can we do to serve our students well? How can we get *better* at meeting the needs of our students? As leaders, how can we have a *greater* impact on team members, clients and stakeholders?

A commentator on Ignatian spirituality, Andy Otto, writes of *magis* as the "spirit of restless desire for greater things." Thus, *magis* can mean looking at your current state with humility and honesty – and maybe a bit of dissatisfaction – but with great confidence that you and your colleagues can make it better.

Magis and other elements of Ignatian spirituality focus on developing a deeper understanding of ourselves – to become, in the words of Jesuit priest and writer James Martin, "bigger souled people." Discovery and becoming "bigger souled" are clearly as much about exploring our inner lives as the outside world. So, appropriately, I close this chapter not with an anecdote or a conclusion, but with questions for your reflection:

Are fears of jerks, stalls, and bumps preventing you from learning something you care about?

Are you more focused on creating "light bulb moments" or finding the "light switch" in your students or colleagues?

How can you strengthen discovery as an element of your decision-making as a leader?

Do you pose questions of your colleagues from a position of humility or authority?

How can you strengthen the interrogative culture of your organization?

How are you connecting with audiences whose questions are important to hear?

What questions are you afraid to pose to yourself or to your colleagues?

CHAPTER EIGHT

IMAGINE

By 2004 I had experienced, as a student and educator, many opening days of schools. But this one was different. As students arrived for the first time that school year, I had a bad case of the first-day-of-school jitters, something I hadn't faced for years.

Walking the halls of the school, I found, calmed my nerves a bit. I greeted staff members, while a local newspaper reporter followed me around, posing an occasional question. We noted upper class students exchanging hugs, happy and optimistic, as they reconnected with their friends. We also saw a few confused freshmen trying to find their home rooms. I could relate to the anxiety in their eyes. I was still in my 30s, with no previous experience as a principal, now leading South Brunswick High School, one of the largest schools in the state.

I helped the younger students find their way as best I could and picked up trash here and there, just as I would for every first day of school for the next seven years. Despite the jitters, I was filled with excitement and hope about this new, awesome responsibility. I was eager to get the year started.

Inevitably, though, the "honeymoon" of the start of every school year wears off as the leaves and the temperatures fall. The buoyancy of September can turn into a day-to-day grind. The happy optimistic glow of the opening of the school year in 2004, however, grew into something much more disturbing in the following weeks, confirming what I'd been told by a number of teachers as I started my new position.

The hallways of the school, as September progressed, grew more noticeably unpleasant. There were too many students wandering the halls when they should have been in class, I noticed. Some of them were blatantly disrespectful toward teachers and peers.

This didn't make sense. The tangible unease I experienced when I walked the halls didn't seem to line up with the school's achievements and reputation. It shouldn't have been that way. The school building was less than ten years old, and a spacious annex had recently opened to accommodate enrollment growth. Computer labs were plentiful, and the facility felt first-class.

Responsible parents in the community also reinforced the importance of education with their motivated children. The school was six miles from Princeton University and 12 miles from Rutgers. Many parents worked at those schools or commuted to New York. SAT scores were solid and the drop-out rate extremely low. The vast majority of students met state assessment standards. On paper, the school looked as good, if not better than it ever had.

But there were serious problems with the school's culture. I noted issues of disrespect, spiteful behavior, and a lack of accountability. Some students knew that the anonymity of a large school enabled them to get away with whatever they wanted.

At the start of each day in the first weeks of school, I was troubled by the dozens of tardy students who lined up outside the attendance secretary's office – because getting to school late had few real consequences at the time. Those students, many of them repeat offenders, missed as much of a third of their first class of the day.

Few faculty members in those days, I also noted, stood at their classroom doorways between classes. They realized that if they did they'd be thrust into confrontations with anonymous students who felt no responsibility to them. If confronted by a faculty member they didn't know, the students would just run off into the massive flow of students down the hall, unlikely to be spotted again. A number of teachers lobbied for me to require students wear IDs like staff members did in order to fight the anonymity.

Even I disliked walking the halls. Every time students passed from class to class, I didn't have to walk far to hear words of animosity and derogatory language. Teachers were understandably on edge – and the way that a few faculty members spoke to students mirrored the tension of the building.

I was also concerned when I learned that freshmen feared they would be harassed in the senior hallway, so they simply avoided it. I was also troubled that a couple of groups of boys tried to establish their own "turf." I remember one spot on the third floor where some students, all bigger than me, gathered to monopolize an already very crowded hallway. They were asserting their dominance by staking out their spot and making other students walk around them as a form of intimidation. When I confronted them, they barely acknowledged me, pausing just long enough to prove they could, and only then moved on.

The situation was so concerning that one teacher described the hallways as the "kids' domain" while the classroom was the "teachers' domain." To confidants, I described it as the "inmates trying to run the asylum."

But there was more. On a street corner directly across from the main entrance, a few yards off school property, students got in their last smoke of the day in full view of parents and buses dropping off other students in the morning. When the smokers needed a cigarette in the middle of the day, they didn't even feel the need to sneak around. They lit up in a third-floor boys' bathroom in the middle of a number of classrooms. Smoke regularly wafted into the classrooms, sending the message that the administration was impotent or even incompetent. It drove me crazy.

One specific conversation I had with a student's father crystallized for me how much work we had ahead of us. His son, a responsible, friendly student-athlete, would avoid the school's bathrooms from the time he arrived at school until the school day ended because of the chaos of those parts of the school with the least adult supervision. This was infuriating, and, even though I was new to the school, I felt I had personally let down the young man.

Even the meetings of the school's Management Team – the group of leaders responsible for the learning environment – reflected the tense tenor of the school. A few of the departmental leaders openly scoffed at their colleagues as tears were occasionally shed over idiotic or even aggressive comments. The alphas in the group tried to intimidate the others. As the year progressed, I cancelled many of the group's meetings because I grew tired of policing the very people who were supposed to be exemplars our values.

Only because of the good work of individual teachers did high levels of teaching and learning continue. Within the four walls of their classrooms, teachers could maintain positive climates where students could relax and learn. While issue after issue swirled in the hallways, good things still happened inside classrooms. Those teachers had a strong vision for learning, and they made it happen. I was inspired by their example.

Deeply disturbed by everything I experienced in our hallways and Management Team meetings, I began to imagine a very different culture for the school. I envisioned a school where students felt safe to be themselves, where all students could find a home. I wanted to lead a school characterized by high expectations, respect, and kindness.

Along with the assistant principals and other leaders in the school, I began the hard work to create a very different kind of school.

Spring 2011. It was 7:29, and the bell to start the first class of the day was about to ring. A good majority of students were already in their classroom, checking the Smart Board for the day's "Do Now," the simple question or task teachers used to get students thinking as they settled in. Many teachers were at their doors greeting students as they entered their classrooms. Nearly eight years had passed from my first school day as principal in 2004.

On the corner across from school, there were no students smoking – that had ended a couple of years ago when I started what we jokingly called the "Chill Patrol." Every day an administrator would stand on that corner, essentially taking back the turf from the smokers.
We also used some technology we purchased, a monitor that detected the flash of a lighter, to crack down on smoking in bathrooms.

We had recently hosted a number of visitors who were interested in what we had accomplished. A representative from the Washington, D.C.-based Character Education Partnership came to assess our application for national recognition. She noted our respectful students, the well-kept facility, and the fact that even in such a big school the staff members seemed to call every student by name.

Other visitors wanted to learn about our effective use of the block schedule with 88-minute classes or our thriving student leadership programs. When speaking to the visitors, I always insisted that, despite our progress, we still had "dusty corners." We were proud of our progress, but constantly aware of what still needed to be done. Like every public high school, a few students still skipped class, others got into squabbles over social media postings, and there were still occasional physical altercations. Our work was not done.

But on most days, as the 7:30 bell rang, I would be concluding my walk from my first-floor office to the furthest corner of the school on the third floor of the annex. Within seconds of the start of the school day, the halls were clear and teachers were already engaging students' minds.

As I took those walks late in my tenure as principal and passed by our music rooms, I couldn't help but be drawn to musical metaphors. It was natural for me to liken the school to a skilled orchestra. Throughout the three floors of the school, expert teachers created beautiful harmonies with their students no matter what the subject. As the conductor on mornings like that, I felt I could step away from the podium, put down my baton, stand back, and just enjoy the music.

That harmony, I readily acknowledge, happened because of the leadership of dozens of adults who worked in the school – from assistant principals to departmental supervisors to teacher-leaders to athletic coaches and even to student-leaders who helped reshape the negative climate of the school in 2004. Through their persistent efforts toward a different vision, they built and sustained a very different school.

We made it happen because we worked together. I was responsible, with the input of many stakeholders, for shaping the school's vision and expectations. Other school leaders who had no interest in perpetuating the status quo of 2004 were empowered to do more. They earned more autonomy to execute changes they sought in their own programs and departments. In addition, over time, we hired several new administrators who shared our collective vision for change and further added to our momentum forward.

After that visit by the representative from the Character Education Partnership, the efforts of all of these leaders were rightfully recognized. In May of 2011, SBHS was designated a

National School of Character, one of only four high schools in the nation so honored that year. We had, indeed, come a long way.[15]

WHEN IMAGINATION FAILS

Thanks to the hard work of many talented educators, we made great progress at SBHS during my tenure as principal. A number of leaders in the school envisioned important changes and made them happen. Unfortunately, too many high schools persistently look like SBHS in 2004. Unlike the leaders at SBHS, educators at those schools accept the status quo. In their hearts, they don't believe things can be different. As a result, students and teachers pass their days disengaged awaiting the final countdown to summer break. They fundamentally suffer from a failure of imagination. Administrators ignore the voice that exists in every real leader that says, "Things can be different – better – if you only try."

There's an inexhaustible list, unfortunately, of schools and other organizations that suffer from unimaginative leadership. Failures of imagination can result in real consequences for students, bad customer service, and even catastrophe.

One high school I visited bragged of high passing rates on state tests. They failed to imagine that they had a glaring problem, like the one I noted when nearly all the students who failed the state test in a given year had Latino, Vietnamese, or Russian surnames.

Earlier in my career, I knew a principal who failed to realize that a "good" kid in his school with solid grades could graduate without learning all that much. The reality was that students with average achievement in that high school could skate through their education with few challenges and little rigor. I learned of one student there who spent 168 minutes per school day in physical education and weightlifting classes.

---

[15] Under the strong leadership of Principal Peter Varela, my successor, Activities Director Lauren Morris, and Student Council Advisor Kelly Boyer, South Brunswick High School's National School of Character designation was renewed in 2017.

Other students in the school, many of them college bound, earned half-credits for running errands and photocopying.

When I was stuck trying to retrieve my luggage after flights in Philadelphia were cancelled because of a snowy Nor'easter, my airline couldn't imagine what a positive customer experience would look like in such a situation. Hundreds of customers lined up outside the airline's baggage office, where only two or three employees toiled away. No managers from the airline were in sight. No one bothered to answer the questions of the weary travelers in line.[16]

Clearly, though, the most catastrophic failure of imagination in contemporary history occurred in the years and months leading up to 9/11. In their final report, the National Commission on the Terrorist Attacks on the United States (the "9/11 Commission") identified four areas of failure that placed the nation in a vulnerable position in 2001: policy, capabilities, management *and imagination*.

Prior to 9/11, senior intelligence and military officials failed to imagine a hijacked aircraft as a weapon. They failed to take note of analysts' reports from the Federal Aviation Administration and the North American Aerospace Defense Command years before that suggested the possible danger. Unfortunately, the 9/11 Commission found, leaders failed to "flesh out and test those scenarios, then figure out a way to turn a scenario into constructive action."

In each of these examples, leaders operated with old assumptions and failed to envision different realities. They failed to exercise one of their most important resources as leaders – their imagination.

---

[16] Ironically, once I got to my destination, I had the opposite experience. While I waited in a short line to check in at the Nationwide Hotel and Conference Center in Lewis Center, Ohio, a staff member approached me, apologized for the wait, and asked if she could answer any questions while I waited to get to the counter. Well done!

I-M-P-U-T-E?

As a youngster, my dad would occasionally test me with words he encountered in his reading, a ritual that left a lasting imprint. His affection for words inspired a love for language that persists today.

That's why I was intrigued when reading a section of Walter Isaacson's *Steve Jobs*. Isaacson described "The Apple Marketing Philosophy," an influential document written in the earliest years of Apple. The document was part of a business plan that Jobs had commissioned consultant Mark Markkula to draw up for the new company.

Markkula identified three clear areas of emphasis for the future of the company: Empathy, focus, and. . .impute? Empathy and focus make sense: Know your customers and their needs and make certain the company maintains a clear sense of its highest-leverage priorities. But impute?

From my reading I knew of impute as a pejorative version of "attribute" (for example, "*We should be wary of imputing a rowdy reputation for British soccer fans from a few unruly hooligans*"). But Markkula used the word's less popular definition to get Jobs and his colleagues to think about how customers develop broader opinions from their experiences with products.

"People *DO* judge a book by its cover," Markkula wrote. Apple might have the best product, the highest quality, the most useful software, etc. But if the company presented them in a slipshod manner, the product will be perceived as slipshod. If the company presents products in a creative, professional manner, customers will *impute* the desired qualities.

Markkula makes it clear that consumers are not coldly rational when they assess the value of a company's projects. Their opinions are not just shaped from data they collect when using a MacBook or an iPhone. Their feelings are also derived from the product's packaging and the look and feel of the Apple store where they're purchased. With "empathy" and "impute" in mind forty years later, the design of Apple products still conveys those clear messages: style, ease of use, and superb engineering.

Organizations, not just products, are designed – sometimes intentionally, sometimes haphazardly. As I encounter the "design" of organizations, I think about the many ways they *impute* meaning.

Trader Joe's, by very intentional design, gets better retail employees by paying them a bit more and encouraging a fun, friendly atmosphere for shopping. Shoppers see Trader Joe's as a more pleasant shopping experience than their local mega-grocery store and as a result impute greater value to Trader Joe's products.

A different message. In contrast is the consistent experience I've had visiting the headquarters of two large school districts. I've witnessed uniformed guards speaking in impatient tones to parents who spoke marginal English. They typically barked "Next" when it was time for the next person to come to the counter followed by a gruff "I.D." I've seen security staff repeatedly treat visitors rudely when they were confused or misunderstood directions. It wouldn't matter what the school district's literacy scores or graduation rates are after that experience. One would easily impute that the district didn't value treating people as humans from the moment they stepped through their doors. A parent might wonder how children get treated in those districts' schools after those types of encounters.

I had a similar experience visiting a high school in New Jersey when I was interviewing for the position of principal in early 2004. I arrived in the principal's office to check in when I found piles of papers on the counter and dozens of dusty trophies on the shelves. Needing a bathroom break I was directed to a boys' bathroom. I immediately noted empty soap dispensers and graffiti all over the bathroom stalls – and this is the bathroom they recommended that a finalist for principal use! Was this the cleanest bathroom in the building? Clearly, this was a school where disrespect toward property was tolerated, and adults in the building didn't care enough to change the culture. The vacuum of leadership was palpable. I imagined a different future for the school as I started the interview. But, alas, they didn't hire me.

As principal at SBHS, I was teasingly called "meticulous." When I saw weeds in the landscaping on the way into school, I'd let the head custodian know. When I saw outdated extracurricular posters in the hallways, I'd take them down myself. When I saw dusty athletic trophies outside the gym, the Athletic Director got a call. I didn't want parents and community members imputing a lackadaisical attitude toward our students' education by impressions of a run-down facility. Nor did I want our students imputing poor value to their education because we didn't take care of the modern facility that the community so generously provided to us.

My attempts at imputing the importance of education haven't always been successful, however. When I was starting my administrative career in Minnesota, I met with a student in my orderly, clean office to assign him a detention for skipping a class. I was new to the school, and I could tell he was feeling me out.

"Why do you dress like a lawyer?" he asked me abruptly.

"You mean the tie and the sport coat? Because I believe I have a really important job ensuring that you get a great education. That's probably more important than what most lawyers do. I want students to know how seriously I take my job. Your education is important to us."

"Oh. Right." the student grunted, unimpressed by my brief soliloquy. "Are we done?"

Organizations and leaders who take Mike Markkula's focus on "impute" seriously think about all the ways that consumers experience their products and services. They intentionally imagine what it would be like to visit a school, call a customer service line, or walk into a hotel room. They think about all the messages conveyed by attractive signage, cleanliness, and politeness of employees – and how all those shape impressions of the brand. Good organizations generate enthusiasm and loyalty as their customers impute great value from their interactions.

RE-IMAGINING

> "We do not need magic to change the world.
> We carry all the power we need inside ourselves already;
> we have the power to imagine better."
> – J.K. Rowling, author of the *Harry Potter* novels

No matter what their purpose, it's easy for organizations to get trapped in pre-existing images of what organizations do. You might think of

- A training program for principals where participants sit in a school library drinking stale coffee as they're lectured to by a speaker who's never really led anything.

- An entertainment company that follows "tried and true" approaches that never surprise customers who attend its events.
- A school choir standing rigidly in place never experiencing the emotion behind the music.

Fortunately for us, three very different vision-driven organizations have escaped these traps and re-imagined their work.

Re-imagining leadership development. The Philadelphia Academy of School Leaders (Philly School Leaders) is driven by a vision for improved student outcomes in a city where academic achievement has been largely stagnant for years. By investing in the development and retention of principals, Philly School Leaders seeks to re-imagine the role and influence of principals. The organization, which I led during its inaugural years, 2015-2017, believes that principal leadership is the critical lever for dramatically improving the quality of schools in Philadelphia.

Philly School Leaders' origins lie in the aspirations of philanthropists Joe Neubauer and Jeanette Lerman-Neubauer to make a difference in the lives of Philadelphia's schoolchildren. A long-time CEO of the Aramark Corporation, Joe knows the value of front-line leaders like school principals. At the basis of the Neubauers' investment is Joe's insistence that "There are no first-rate schools without first-rate leaders." Joe and Jeanette envision Philadelphia as a city where the best principals

- Continue to grow in their effectiveness.
- Remain steadfast in their commitment to Philadelphia schools.
- Help other principals get better.

Through the generosity of the Neubauer Family Foundation, Philly School Leaders is able to provide a first-class experience for principals selected for the prestigious Neubauer Fellowship in Educational Leadership. This experience includes intensive institutes with accomplished experts in corporate-quality conference facilities. The principals also meet in small groups with corporate and civic leaders, who have included Brian Roberts, CEO of Comcast, and Madeline Bell, president of the world-class Children's Hospital of Philadelphia. The Neubauers see principals as important as corporate leaders – if not more so – and they make certain they are treated that way.

In order to ensure the best possible experience for Neubauer Fellows, our staff took time to envision the "user experience" of the Fellowship from end to end. We wanted principals' participation to be effortless so they felt valued and important. We wouldn't tolerate any barriers to their learning. At our staff meetings before big events like our Summer Institute, I'd have our team walk through the schedule from the perspective of a participant:

Do I know exactly where I should park?

Will it be easy to find the meeting space from the parking garage?

Will I encounter a friendly, knowledgeable face as I walk into the first session?

Will the session be relevant and informative?

As a result of this careful preparation, we earned superb scores on participant surveys after our programs.

Like an Apple customer imputing value for a sleek new MacBook as she opens the crisp, white box, we wanted principals to impute more value to their role because of the way they were treated during the Fellowship. If they perceived themselves to be valued and important leaders, then they would more likely stay in Philadelphia and make an even bigger impact. Nearly three years into its existence, the organization has helped to retain more than 90% of participating educational leaders in the city, a significant accomplishment in any urban setting.

Philly School Leaders re-imagines the education sector in Philadelphia as a hub for developing, attracting, and retaining the best principals in the country and seeks to establish the role of principal as much more substantial the just managing a school building. The Neubauers and the Philly School Leaders team seek to ensure that the city sees principals as they do – as significant and influential leaders worthy of the city's respect and investment.

Re-imagining entertainment. In the century or so after Barnum and Bailey and the Ringling brothers began staging their shows, the circus reflected their vision of dancing bears, goofy clowns, fearless lion tamers, and a few acrobats under the big top. In the late 1970s, however, an innovative *Quebecois* artist and his compatriots began to reconsider the circus. Guy Laliberte at the time was an accordionist, stilt-walker and fire-eater with a taste for travel and art.

Laliberte and a group of fellow street performers first joined creative forces in Baie-Saint-Paul, a small artsy city northeast of Quebec City. They performed locally, earning a loyal group of fans. But Laliberte had a bold vision beyond the artistic enclave.

That vision drove Laliberte, in 1984, to lobby the Quebec provincial government for initial funding of his dream. As a result of his persistence, the unusual group of performers was awarded a $1 million contract to develop a celebration for the 450th anniversary of the discovery of Canada. The contract enabled Laliberte to create a new show that utilized the diverse talents of his friends and launch a tour throughout the province. The new *cirque* had no animals; it was a new mixture of culture, art, and acrobatic grace under the circus tent. Because the sun represented youth, energy and strength, Laliberte named the endeavor *Cirque du Soleil*. The Cirque tour of Quebec earned them more fans and attention, but they continued to struggle to find firm financial footing until a 1987 tour of the U.S. earned them investors and a sustainable future.

Despite the rapid growth of the company in the 1990s, Laliberte continued to serve as Cirque's disciplined, perfectionist creative force. Cirque shows became known for their distinctive blending of world cultures and circus styles from around the globe.

By the summer of 2002, when I attended my first Cirque show, *Alegria*, the company had eight shows. Five were touring the globe with two based in Las Vegas, and one in residence at Disney World.

I had seen highlights of a show or two on television, but the medium clearly hadn't done justice to the entire sensory experience of Cirque. I was impressed, if not astounded, by the near-perfect performance and the high standards underlying it – from storytelling to music to humor to artistry. Laliberte's strong vision for artistic perfection was evident, and the creative leadership of that particular production, Franco Dragone and Gilles Ste-Croix, built on it.

I was hooked after *Alegria*. As of today, I've seen about ten Cirque shows, several more than once. After that first show, I read and watched everything about Cirque that I could get my hands on.

Through that process, I've come to appreciate three particular hallmarks of Cirque's success:

- **A bold creative vision.** Cirque accepts no limits to its creative process, drawing on the arts, diverse cultures, nature, science, and sports.
- **Relentless pursuit of precision and perfection.** Discipline, practice, and hard work are clearly part of the ethos of Cirque.
- **Indefatigable pursuit of talent.** Cirque never accepts second-best in its casts, creative teams, or the units that support them. They recruit internationally for the best talent.

Cirque continues to use these three approaches to great success. As of early 2018, the company had 21 active shows touring or in residence. In total, Cirque has entertained more than 160 million spectators on six continents. Though still involved in the creative direction of the company, Laliberte sold much of his stake in 2015. The former stilt-walker and fire-breather is now among the wealthiest people in the world.

Re-imagining the chorus. The children who live in the Graniteville, Staten Island neighborhood of New York Public School 22 (P.S. 22) are just like the kids who go to public schools in every other city in the nation. They can be charming and squirrelly, responsible and forgetful, just like kids anywhere.

In many ways, P.S. 22 looks like thousands of other urban schools. It's not a magnet school. It's not a special school. It's a neighborhood school where students represent all the beautiful hues of our nation's ethnicities. Ninety percent of students are people of color. A quarter of its students receive special education support. About a third of its students are absent often enough that it has an impact on their education. Most students in the school struggle to meet state academic standards in the school.

Since the year 2000, Gregg Breinberg has shared his infectious passion for music with the students of P.S. 22, particularly the fifth-grade chorus he founded. Breinberg re-imagined the idea of an elementary school choir. It was no longer about students standing stiffly on risers in starched white shirts singing the usual fare. Instead, Mr. B, as his students affectionately call him, let them sing songs they knew. And he introduced them to new songs they grew to love.

Students love Mr. B's enthusiasm. He encourages them to *feel* the music – to move and sway and gesture as they experienced the music they sing. "Music is a whole-body experience," Breinberg says. "I just don't believe in choreographed performances," the director explains. "For me, music should inspire individual and natural movement, and that's what these kids bring to their performances."

In their early years, the chorus earned a local following. Audiences took note of the director's novel approach. Parents loved seeing their sons and daughters so passionate about music. Word of the chorus began to spread throughout Staten Island.

As the reputation of the Chorus grew, a friend suggested that Breinberg post videos of the students' take on contemporary songs on YouTube, which at the time was just catching on with kids and Millennials. Most of the early posts were from the Chorus's concert performances, but YouTube views began to take off when Breinberg posted the chorus's now distinctive, simple style: Students seated in the hard wood seats of their school's simple auditorium, swaying and singing. A single camera captured the smiling faces of the adorable performers. After Tori Amos songs like "Dragon" and "Bouncing Off Clouds" earned thousands of hits, virtual word-of-mouth began to earn the Chorus a dedicated fandom. In subsequent years, the chorus's rendition of Adele's "Rolling in the Deep" and Leonard Cohen's "Hallelujah" have each earned more than 2 million views each – and Lady Gaga's "Just Dance" more than five million. To date, the P.S. 22 Chorus videos have been viewed more than 75 million times. The group's popularity isn't lost on the kids. As one Chorus member said, "I totally went from nobody to somebody."

Breinberg's leadership has afforded the city kids truly amazing experiences. The group's web popularity has earned them many special audiences and collaborators. They've performed for President Obama and appeared on *Good Morning America* and the *Today Show*. They've sung with Carrie Underwood, Katy Perry, and dozens of other well-known musicians. In perhaps their most memorable performance, they stole the show at the 2011 Academy Awards singing "Somewhere Over the Rainbow."

These are truly unique opportunities for students from Graniteville. "These are kids who are humble children. They don't come from magnificent backgrounds," Breinberg explains.

Breinberg has not only won the admiration of the entertainment industry, but leaders in other realms have come to appreciate what he's accomplished. The billionaire and three-time New York Mayor Michael Bloomberg, for example, calls Breinberg "a great teacher but also. . .a great leader."

Mr. B remains humble about the success of the Chorus. "Who else has that kind of luck" Breinberg says, "that they can go to work and be happier for going to work?"

"It's just great being able to provide these experiences. It's always exciting to see the kids get excited about the music, and that's the most important thing."

Lessons from Re-Imagining. The success of these three very different organizations – Philly School Leaders, Cirque du Soleil, and the P.S. 22 Chorus – clearly indicates we have much to learn from them. Here are three key lessons:

Work from a new template. Breinberg looked to pop music, not traditional elementary school choirs, for inspiration for the Chorus. Philly School Leaders rejected old models of professional development in education, wanting their programs to resemble, if not exceed, corporate programs.

Fight for your vision. When the P.S. 22 chorus rehearsed for the 2011 Academy Awards, the directors wanted students to limit their gestures and stand still. Breinberg politely fought for allowing the students – and the chorus – to be themselves, and he won! When funds proved scarce for Laliberte's creative vision in 1983, he personally lobbied the Quebec government officials for a million-dollar grant, and he won!

Listen to your customers and clients. Both Philly School Leaders and Cirque constantly gather data about "customer satisfaction." Philly School Leaders surveys participants after every event ensure that logistics and program content are always on target.

URGENCY

In 1984, Guy Laliberte had a bold vision and a powerful sense of urgency. He had a plan and stories he wanted to tell. He was prepared to persist through artistic and financial ups and downs in order to bring his vision to life. Imaginative leaders like Laliberte see every passing day as another day their vision isn't realized.

In contrast are leaders who lack a powerful vision and the urgency that comes from it. A couple of years ago, I visited a humane, pleasant school located in a tough neighborhood in Philadelphia. Many students were impacted by one or more social maladies – poverty, violence, mental illness and addiction. The majority of the students performed well below state averages in math and language arts. Many students were three or more grade levels behind in reading.

Educators in the school were kind, caring people, and the school appeared to be a humane refuge for students from the dangers of the neighborhood. But when it came to ensuring that students had the skills they needed for college or a career – or even graduating from high school, I saw little urgency at the school.

I recall one moment when a group of children lined up in the hallway after a bathroom break as their teacher and the principal chatted. The students were well behaved, if not bored. A few fidgeted; several chattered quietly. The class's teacher chatted amiably with the school's principal for several minutes. The clock in my head tick-tick-ticked the seconds, then minutes, of lost instructional time.

I was just a visitor, but wanted to say to both educators, "Get these kids back to their classroom. They should be learning, not listening to your stupid conversation. These kids are counting on you."

I wanted to hear the principal say, "Hey, I know you want to get started with your next lesson. I'll walk with your students back to your room and help them get settled while you start the lesson. Every minute of learning counts. Right, students?!" But that's not what happened.

Leaders and organizations express their values in how they use time. Clearly, this school didn't feel the sense of urgency that they should have.

More effective schools have powerful sense of urgency. They utilize the school day as effectively as possible. Teachers at SBHS, for example, were expected to conduct "bell-to-bell instruction," and that largely happened. Teachers rightfully complained when interruptions interfered with their treasured instructional time.

The school's administrative team played a part, too. Before school, we typically walked the halls to ensure students got to class on time. As I walked the halls, students frequently rolled their eyes as their nerdy principal repeated, "So little time, so much to learn! Let's get to class!" But at least they knew what our values were.

I left the principalship in 2012, and experienced urgency in a very different line of work. I was excited to work with Christopher Cerf, who then served as New Jersey's Commissioner of Education. Cerf encouraged his senior leaders to take advantage opportunities to make good education policy when they presented themselves. In leading the Department's work on teacher and principal evaluation, we knew that the window of opportunity for policy change wouldn't remain open forever, and it didn't. We moved quickly in 2012-2013 and earned passage of a landmark set of regulations that transformed educator evaluation in the state.

Leaders, like Cerf, who seek to create an enduring don't imagine a future that *might change*. They imagine a future that *will* change. As a result, they act with urgency. As I noted in Chapter 5, military leaders operate in a "vulnerable, uncertain, complex, and ambiguous" environment. They know they must strike quickly when they are afforded an opportunity. Companies also know that markets don't last forever. They must act with urgency knowing that the marketplace can change rapidly, especially since the advent of the Information Age. The best companies understand that they must execute quickly and well with a constant eye on the future.

FAITH, HOPE AND REALISM

The late Admiral Jim Stockdale, a Congressional Medal of Honor winner and a true American hero, deserves more recognition. Stockdale was imprisoned in the famous Vietnamese prison known as the "Hanoi Hilton" for eight horrible years after the plane he was piloting was shot down. There he was tortured more than 20 times. In *Good to Great,* Jim Collins shares what

Stockdale told him about hope during those eight years. "You must never confuse faith that you will prevail in the end," Stockdale said, "with the discipline to confront the most brutal facts of your current reality, whatever they might be." Stockdale clearly imagined being free from his captor and reunited with his family, but he remained deeply realistic about the moment at hand. Collins termed this the "Stockdale paradox."

High-performing organizations and leaders live by the Stockdale Paradox. They believe they will, in the end, be successful. But they never shy away from the current reality. Leaders with an impact understand the good, bad, and ugly about their organizations. These leaders don't sweep things under the rug. They readily acknowledge the "dusty corners" of organizations. All organizations – companies, non-profits, churches, even families – have them. They're the nagging little problems or unfinished business that leaders identify. Leaders may not have the time and resources to get to all nagging organizational dust bunnies, but they know where they are and they've prioritized which corner to attack next.

One of my favorite fictional coaches, Eric Taylor of *Friday Night Lights*, shared a similar message with his team. Coach Taylor's pep talks and locker room posters reminded players, "*Clear eyes. Full hearts. Can't Lose.*" Through the five seasons of the show, the meaning of the mantra becomes clear:

- *Clear eyes.* Keep an uncompromising vision of your current reality and a clarity of purpose.
- *Full hearts.* Believe in your own and the team's abilities. Love your teammates as brothers.
- *Can't lose.* You may not win every game, but with clear eyes and full hearts, you'll win and win often. Even when you don't win, you *can't lose.* You'll walk off the field proud of yourself and your teammates.

Like the Dillon Panthers, effective organizations must, with "clear eyes," acknowledge current realities, remain optimistic with "full hearts," and hold firmly to a "can't lose" vision for success.

EXCELLENCE

I was never much of an athlete growing up. I made the seventh and eighth grade basketball teams just because I was a nice kid who hustled. As a point of pride, in seventh grade I eventually made it up to being the seventh man off the bench. Or was it eighth?

My athletic exploits as a kid were pretty limited. Oddly enough, my drive to be excellent didn't spill over to my jump shot or even getting better on the trombone. But the academic world was somewhat different.

I recall one moment from my student days when I was in a huge panic. Minutes before the school bus was to pull up to my stop, I realized something was missing from my folder for school. My teacher had assigned some math homework, which I had dutifully completed. That morning, however, the sheet was nowhere to be found. I knew I had done it. I *always* did my homework.

I ran from counter to counter in a panic looking for the sheet with the slightly frayed edges after being torn from the workbook. Exasperated, I even raced to the cabinets where the photo albums were kept and rifled through a small pile of papers there. No luck.

Panic spread throughout my body as my mother told me, "It's okay. These things happen. You're always responsible." But I couldn't show up at school without my work! Near tears, my hands shaking, I simply wasn't ready to face the day without that sheet of math problems. I was desperate. I was seven years old.

I might just be hard-wired that way. I have always been painfully aware when my work doesn't hit the mark. I've never been satisfied with "good enough." When I'm in a leadership role, I hate knowing someone is doing something better than I am. For me, it's less about competitiveness and more about doing my best work. It's that feeling that I've hit the target that I set for myself – not one of the outer rings, but the bullseye.

This idea of taking on a difficult task and then hitting the target is captured by the ancient Greek word *arête*. The word doesn't have a direct translation, but it denotes a variety of sentiments around excellence – things like moral virtue, purpose, and effectiveness. The concept makes strong connections between doing good work and living a good life. *Arête* was emphasized in the *paideia,* the preparation of boys for manhood that included physical, mental and spiritual training. Boys in the privileged classes were taught the importance of achieving *arête* in each domain.

Jim Collins' conception of the Level 5 leader is not too far off the mark from the Greek conception of *arête*. The most effective leaders possess admirable personal characteristics, but also an eagerness to do great work. Level 5 leaders are ambitious for their organizations. They constantly imagine ways that the organization can get better. They're never satisfied.

Great school and district leaders are driven by their own notions of *arête*. They doggedly look for ways to stretch their students to even higher levels of achievement. As they pursue excellence, imaginative leaders in these and other great school districts pose questions like these:

- Who's performing better than us?
- Who's getting results that exceed expectations? Who's beating the odds?
- What can we learn from these schools?

Leaders who pose questions like these focus their organizations on the relentless pursuit of excellence. They strive, in business author Seth Godin's words, to "make things worth talking about." There's a boldness in their confidence and their will to make amazing things happen. They hear the voice of Daniel Burnham, creator of iconic buildings and city plans, in their head: "Make no little plans, they have no magic to stir men's blood."[17]

IMAGINATION AND STEWARDSHIP

Leaders with vision and imagination are driven not only by the pursuit of excellence, but also by creating excellence that persists. They feel accountable to future generations. As some may remember from Girl Scouts or Boy Scouts, they feel responsible for "leaving the campsite better than you found it."

As James Kerr describes in his book *Legacy: What the All Blacks Can Teach Us about the Business of Life*, the success of the New Zealand men's national rugby team is shaped by the Maori view of *whakapapa*. This concept emphasizes the interdependence of all of

---

[17] Burnham designed two of my favorite structures, the Flatiron Building in New York and Union Station in Washington, D.C. He was also Director of Works for the 1893 World's Columbian Exposition, which is richly described in Erik Larson's excellent book *Devil in the White City: Murder, Magic and Madness at the Fair that Changed America*.

creation – and of the members of the team. It reminds the All Blacks of their genealogy and their "place in the ascending order of all living things." Knowing one's place in an interconnected world places responsibility on those living – or on those wearing the All Blacks' emblem today.

Leaders with this perspective see themselves as stewards of a tradition. They are temporary caretakers of an organization or community with a strong sense of responsibility to leave it healthy and vibrant. This is the antithesis of the self-serving leader who focuses only on the interests of himself and his "tribe."

Because of their imaginations, leaders with a strong sense of stewardship are able to combine both a strong urgency to effect positive change in the present and an understanding that fostering excellence takes time. They are realistic about their current realities, but deeply hopeful about the future. Impatient as they seek to make their vision real, these leaders feel it is their duty to invest personally and organizationally in a future they may not even see.

The concepts of duty and stewardship are, unfortunately, not part of the contemporary lingo of books on the business bestseller list, but they remain timeless. Leaders who seek to create an enduring impact are deeply humbled by the responsibility that stewardship entails – and they're excited by the responsibility. They are driven by the potential to be a part of a lasting legacy, not short-term gains. They see service to those who follow them as a privilege, not a burden.

CHAPTER NINE

DARE

The lights grew dim in a crowded high school gymnasium. About 2,000 teenagers shifted restlessly in anticipation of another uninspiring pep rally. It was the end of the day, classes were over, and the only thing that stood in the way of students and their weekend was the procession of team captains and coaches talking about how optimistic they were about their upcoming seasons.

Posters in the school's black and gold colors covered the walls at the top of the wooden stands with the biggest one dedicated to the seniors, the Class of 2005.

Students and teachers anticipated the usual script as the start of the rally approached. But then, the lights began to dim, plunging 2,000 students into relative darkness. This was different. Unexpected. A few teachers were perturbed and wanted an explanation.

More observant students noticed something else that was different. There was DJ equipment set up on the floor of the gym. Interesting.

Light peaked through the open doors of one corner of the gym. A group of students, dressed entirely in dark clothing, gathered at the doors.

A minute or two passed, and over the chatter of the students, the first plucks and beats of a song began to play. An English teacher known for her gentle demeanor and affection for heavy metal music recognized the song immediately and smiled to herself. Then more teachers – at least those born in the 1960s – recognized the first pulsing chords of one of the most iconic openings in the history of hard rock.

Seconds later, the strains of the lead vocalist started reverberating against a bass beat:

Back in black
I hit the sack
I've been too long I'm glad to be back

As AC/DC's Brian Johnson screeched the lyrics like a cracking whip, the students could see a phalanx of about a dozen girls clad in black athletic clothes begin to strut rhythmically across the gym floor. They were in tight formation, moving slowly and deliberately to the beat of "Back in Black."

Well, I'm back in black
Yes, I'm back in black

As the girls reached center court, they formed a tight circle. A spotlight began to scan the gymnasium. A few students paying close attention in the dim light noticed a figure dressed in black pants and black hoodie emerge from the circle. The girls – yes, they were the cheerleaders – formed a new formation. A few knelt as others took up a spotting position behind them. The hooded figure crouched in the middle of the group, waiting for a cue.

'Cause I'm back on the track
And I'm beatin' the flack

Nearly every student's eyes were on center court. When the vocals reached their zenith, the hooded figure placed his foot in a crouching cheerleader's hands and began to rise upward as another cheerleader supported his other foot.

So look at me now
I'm just makin' my play
Don't try to push your luck, just get out of my way

When the cheerleaders' arms locked him in place nearly eight feet in the air, he kept his body rigid just as he had been coached and tossed back his hood. The spotlight hit his face as his arms pumped in triumph. A few teachers and students gasped in recognition.

"That's the freakin' principal!"

After a few seconds, the captain of the squad uttered the command, and, with a light toss, I flew through the air into the interweaved arms of the cheerleaders forming a basket catch.

The crowd went wild.

The "Back in Black" opening to that pep rally went exactly according to plan. It set a playful tone to the rally that one veteran teacher told me "was the best the school ever had."

But there were many moments as we prepared when serious doubts encroached on my thinking:

You're going to make a fool of yourself.

You're going to come crashing down and either hurt the cheerleaders or yourself.

Is this really the right tone a principal should set?

Do you really want to be the center of attention like this?

The last question nagged at me. I had no fears about speaking to a group of students or parents. That was an important part of my job. But this was different. There were too many variables I couldn't control. Once I almost gave up on the idea after I didn't do so well practicing with the girl despite their encouragement.

Despite my persistent doubts, I knew I had to follow through and be a little daring, and I'm glad I did.

My little cheerleading trick wasn't the only time I took that kind of chance as a leader of a school. For a video promoting a student-faculty game, I shot a series of "air balls" and got stuffed by a six-foot-nine-inch student-athlete who went on to play Division I college basketball. For a history club fundraiser, I allowed students to duct-tape me to a wall. (Yes, I was completely affixed to the wall. Students threatened to leave me there for days.)

I've also had my head completely shaved twice – once as a teacher after my homeroom met a goal for a canned food drive, the second at the conclusion of a post-9/11 fundraiser. I've also taken a pie in the face during a pep rally and spent time in a bone-chilling dunk tank.

I did all of those things not only because I like to have fun, but also to send a strong message to students and staff. Members about my leadership. I could laugh at myself. I don't take myself too seriously. When it came to a good cause, I didn't have to maintain a certain image. I dared to be different from the stereotype of the unapproachable, stuffy principal. I was trying to live by the words I often shared with leaders I've mentored: Take your work, not yourself, seriously.

I wasn't raised to be daring. As children and adolescents, both of my parents had tumultuous family lives with unpredictable fathers. They were socially conservative people who aspired to a quiet, conventional family life, and that's what they created for their children. They cultivated the image of a "shiny happy family." Conflict was squelched. Differences of opinion were not encouraged. When I asserted myself as a youngster, my mother cautioned me not to get "too big for my britches." Those five words irked me more than anything my parents would say. They raised me to be a confident young man but asserting myself with them was off-limits.

Because I grew up in an environment where I was taught to be confident but still felt restricted, I looked for ways to stretch myself. With each decision, I found that I felt more self-assured:

I was the small-town kid who had the audacity to apply to a college that accepts six percent of its applicants.

I was the teetotaling college student who chose to live in a suite with 11 other guys who liked to build pyramids out of empty beer kegs from the parties we hosted.

I was the Ivy League grad who wanted to be a teacher.

I was the serious-minded principal who could laugh at himself and have fun.

I was the progressive Democrat who worked for a Republican governor.

I was the veteran educator who decided to pick up his life, move to a new state, and take on leadership of a start-up.

While advice-giving relatives were telling me to go to law school or, later, to focus on building up a good pension, I've charted my own course. Along the way, I've learned that we can't achieve substantial goals as individuals or as leaders *without* being daring.

As I've learned from my own experiences and those of other leaders, being a daring leader isn't about doing things merely for shock value. It's about

- Leading with audacity.
- Finding your own path.
- Showing you care.
- Challenging the status quo.
- Defying expectations.

By developing these traits, daring leaders can accomplish the significant goals they seek. Let's explore each of these traits.

LEADING WITH AUDACITY

It all started with the 2014 World Cup. In the past, I was a passive fan, catching highlights from World Cup games when the U.S. Men's and Women's soccer teams competed. But as the 2014 competition approached, I found myself drawn in. Engrossed, even. For the first time, I paid attention to the best teams and players. The speed, agility, and gracefulness of James Rodríguez, Thomas Müller, Messi, and Neymar taught me what a compelling sport it was. Years of watching American high school soccer as a teacher and principal hadn't convinced me, as so many claim, that it's the "beautiful game." The 2014 World Cup did. I was hooked.

After Germany's Cup victory that summer, I had to find a new outlet for my budding interest. Under the influence of an English friend, I started watching the Premier League and became a fan of the spunky Tottenham Hotspur led by the young star Harry Kane.

I'm convinced that becoming a Spurs fan might've been destiny (or a fortunate occurrence). While watching one Spurs game with my English friend, I noticed the team's motto emblazoned on signs throughout their stadium. Originally expressed in Latin – *audere est facere* – today it's posted in the vernacular: To Dare is To Do. It's a fitting slogan for a team known for its tradition of playing with flair.

The Spurs' motto immediately resonated with me. In the Spurs' team culture, the motto stresses, there's no room for aloofness or passivity in achieving something phenomenal. Daring is inextricably linked to doing. You can't dare to aspire to win the Champions League, Premier League, or F.A. Cup unless you're getting your kit dirty. You can't be a successful leader achieving your organization's most important goals unless you're fully engaged and, as Theodore Roosevelt said, "in the arena." In a "Dare is to Do" world, talk is cheap.

The roots of the word audacity lie in in the Latin word for dare: *audere*. Daring, audacious leaders are action-oriented with bold, substantial goals. Leaders with audacity aren't content with just getting by. They're never satisfied receiving the runner-up trophy. They set goals that they believe might be just be beyond their reach, and they're determined to achieve them.

As part of our annual character education initiatives at South Brunswick High School, I posed just those kinds of goals for the school community. After Hurricane Katrina, for example, I challenged the school to donate $10,000 for the American Red Cross in about two weeks. After the devastating 2010 earthquake in Haiti, we sought to raise $8,000 in just a few days. And another year, I challenged staff and students to perform more than 6,000 hours of community service in three weeks (about 2 hours per staff member and student). We accomplished the first and second goals but missed the third. While achieving the objectives was important, what I really wanted students to see was my confidence in them to achieve those daring goals and their growing confidence in achieving something truly significant. The result was that students initiated their own service projects with substantial impacts. Success fostered success.

While bold and lofty, the objectives described above might not qualify as Big Hairy Audacious Goals (BHAGs) in the terminology of Jim Collins' business classics *Built to Last* and *Good to Great*. A BHAG "is a huge and daunting goal – like a big mountain to climb. It is clear, compelling, and people 'get it' right away," Collins explains. "A BHAG serves as a unifying focal point of effort, galvanizing people and creating team spirit as people strive toward a finish line."

After eight years as a principal, I joined the staff of the New Jersey Department of Education (NJDOE) for three years. During the third of those years, I served as the Department's Chief Intervention Officer, providing oversight for the 14 districts where the state had some form of formal intervention because of financial mismanagement, poor student achievement, or both. Those districts served about 135,000 students and included Newark, Jersey City, Trenton, and Camden – the kinds of districts that often attract media attention for less than ideal reasons.

During that year, I saw the need to propose a BHAG for my team. In 2015, the NJDOE prepared to launch a new, online student testing system, the Partnership for Assessment for Readiness for College and Careers (PARCC). Fearful of a potential catastrophe in state intervention districts if preparations were inadequate, I charged my small team with the goal of ensuring a smooth implementation of the first year of PARCC in our districts.

This was a significant objective. Most of these districts had aging infrastructures, and many of them struggled with basic compliance and capacity in implementing much less complex initiatives. My deputy at the time, Christopher Snyder, hit the road and conducted in-person readiness assessments in a majority of the districts. Some districts, like Newark, had planned carefully and appeared to be ready. Others were clearly not. As the start of the first statewide online test grew close, Chris and I worked closely with the district leadership, the staff from the NJDOE responsible for implementing PARCC, and a small group of consultants we secured to fill gaps.

As students began to take the PARCC tests for the first time that spring, I eagerly awaited word from our districts. Though there were a few bumps in some places, it was largely "no news was good news." While there were some New Jersey districts that flubbed PARCC implementation, they weren't ours. Our 14 districts stayed out of the headlines that first year of the new assessment, while others got faulted for failures in planning and implementation.

"We had some district problems, but not many," Commissioner of Education (and my boss at the time) Dave Hespe told the media after the first day of PARCC testing. "Far fewer than we expected to be completely candid with you." Thanks to the good work of leaders in districts and the NJDOE, we all got the job done.

After achieving the BHAG, our small team framed a few important lessons from the experience:

- Audacious goals can sometimes lead to disagreements about roles and responsibilities – about who owns what "turf." We didn't give up on our goal when this occurred. We just worked through the issues through communication and mutual respect.

- BHAGs can reveal resource and capacity problems. Before pursuing an audacious goal, be prepared to get creative to address these issues. We were a lean team but managed to find the expertise and funding to fill gaps.
- As a relatively new team, the BHAG clearly established a clear, outcome-based focus for us. This clear purpose proved helpful both to us as a team and to the districts we served.

Like armor. In the premiere episode of *Game of Thrones*, the dwarf Tyrion Lannister, tells the bastard son of Ned Stark, "Never forget what you are; the rest of the world will not. Wear it like armor, and it can never be used to harm you." Tyrion, as the series progresses, becomes a wise, formidable leader, who audaciously wears his traits and trials "like armor."

In my best moments, I've embraced this kind of authenticity as a leader.[18] In most organizations being an authentic leader is itself an audacious act. Leaders are expected to play a role which can often impede their ability to be authentic. Nevertheless, organizations benefit from the daring leader who finds a way to be herself, while still fulfilling the role of leader.

I tried to be authentic as a principal when I shared certain aspects of my life with staff members and students. When a group of student volunteers were being trained to work with senior citizens, for example, I shared my experiences with my mother's progressing dementia.

Similarly, toward the end of my tenure at the high school, I was the guest speaker at the school's Gay-Straight Alliance. I wanted the students to know how much I valued being their openly gay principal, but I was surprised by their reaction. It seemed that my sexual orientation had become old news in the community. "I can't believe you're really gay!" one student said. "We just thought that was just a rumor." Apparently the community had accepted that part of me so much that they had stopped talking about it.

---

[18] See Chapter 6, "Thrive," for further exploration of leadership and authenticity.

FIND YOUR OWN PATH

> So don't let your luggage define your travels
> Each life unravels differently
> And experiences are what make up
> The colours of our tapestry
> – Shane Koyczan, poet and spoken-word artist

College reunions are clearly a mixed bag. Reconnecting with friends and former roommates can be a lot of fun. But reunions can also lead to comparisons: Who's the most accomplished? Who has the most influence? Who's making the most money? And for the guys, who's got the fullest head of hair? Fortunately, I'm doing very well on the last question, but when I attended my 25th college reunion a few years ago I found myself mulling deeply over those other questions.

I was eager to attend the reunion to see my college friends, some of whom were part of an aptly-named 12-person suite known as "The Zoo." I never fail to be humbled by my Princeton friends. There's an MIT professor, an orthopedic surgeon, and an influential literary agent. One has argued a number of cases before the Supreme Court, and several are successful venture capitalists. Among other members of the Princeton Class of 1989 is the founder of Teach for America and the head coach of the Dallas Cowboys. Being surrounded by these intelligent, ambitious people was as important to my college education as my professors were.

Though I wasn't exactly a trailblazer, I chose to follow a less typical path after Princeton. During my senior year, I was heading down the same road as other history majors interested in politics and public policy. I took the LSAT and accumulated a pile of law school brochures. But before I filled out any applications, I realized law school wasn't the right decision for me.

Some key experiences had led me in a different direction. Through my involvement in the Princeton Model Congress, a political simulation for high school students in Washington, D.C., I found out that I enjoyed working with teenagers, and I was good at it. I enjoyed their energy and directness, and they (largely) enjoyed my sense of humor and my insights.

My parents, after investing in my pricey education, were confused. They envisioned me as a lawyer in a sharp suit and wing tips. They saw me as a candidate for mayor or Congressman. Become a teacher? I explained that I loved working with kids – which they knew – and needed more time to sort out my professional plans.

After a few interviews for teaching positions, I finally was hired by my alma mater, St. John's Jesuit High School in Toledo. That decision to jettison my plans for law school set a pattern for the rest of my career. I've always chosen work that interests me – where I feel I can make a difference as a leader.

I've learned that as I've approached decisions in my life I've chosen to march to a slightly different beat. As a young teen, I left a school where I was a big fish in a small pond to go to a better high school where I knew no one. At the start of college, where even at Princeton there was pressure to binge drink, I chose not to drink at all. Only later on, on my own terms, did I start to enjoy a beer here and there.

Continuing to choose my own path continued later in life. I became one of the few openly gay suburban high school principals in the nation. Then, as a tenured high school principal, I gave up job security and a school I loved to lead a controversial education policy initiative. My path, my decision.

At that college reunion several years ago, I marveled at the number of very accomplished Princeton graduates sheepishly asking Cowboys Coach Jason Garrett, who was always gracious, for a photograph with their kids. While I didn't have people lining up to have their picture taken with me, I could tell that my classmates appreciated my career decisions. When I talked to people I hadn't seen for 25 years and told them I had spent my whole career as an educator, their reactions were consistent. Your work is so important, they told me, I'm just a lawyer (or banker or management consultant.) A couple of them expressed their envy, "You get to do something that matters."

On Saturday night of the reunion, needing a respite from the chitchat, I decided to check out the musical headliner for the weekend. It's a Princeton tradition that at significant reunions like the 25th a big-name band performs. For ours, it was hip hop artist Flo Rida. As "Flo" performed, the 47-year-olds from my class flopped around on the dance floor along with younger alumni and graduating seniors who, per tradition, are allowed to crash the party. As I too flopped around, I noticed a familiar younger face dancing to my right. We were both sweaty, bobbing up and down, but I immediately recognized him. I had been his high school principal before he matriculated at Princeton. He yelled, "MR. MATHENEY!" We laughed, high-fived, and got back to dancing.

As I drove home after the party, I thought about the conversations of the night and the moment on the dance floor. Knowing that the school I led had set my former student on a trajectory to achieve his dreams left me with a deep sense of satisfaction. Despite the doubts often sown at college reunions, I knew that I had chosen the right path.

SHOWING YOU CARE

About a decade ago, that path took me to a boys' basketball championship game at the arena on the Rutgers University campus. It was a huge game for us. Hundreds of students filled one end of the stands creating a sea of black and gold.

As the game started, a security guard on the floor of the arena kept an eye on our student section. Noticing one issue she thought she needed to address, she approached an assistant principal who was also keeping an eye on the students above her. "Why is that student over there on the floor of the arena? He's getting a little excited. Why isn't he in the stands with the other students?"

"Which student?" responded the administrator, a bit surprised that she may have missed something.

"The short one over there. In the hoodie and baseball cap," the guard answered.

"Oh. That's not a student. That's our principal."

Yes, I was a bit excitable at times. I fondly remember many of those moments: Feeling emotional highs and lows as the girls' volleyball team competed for county titles. Cheering on future Atlanta Falcon Mohamed Sanu as he passed and ran for touchdowns. Watching in awe from the top of the press box as our exemplary Marching Band wove intricate patterns and made beautiful music. I got excited because I was proud and I cared.

When you work with teenagers every day it's easy for their feigned indifference to rub off on you. The cultures of many organizations – even some schools – unintentionally encourage disengagement, even cynicism. If you don't care, you'll never be disappointed. You'll never experience the highs and lows of those who do care.

In contrast great leaders are *all in*. They care, and they're not afraid to show it. Caring begins with showing up and progresses to enthusiasm. I tried to show students that I cared in a very real way. When the football team scored a touchdown, I joined the cheerleaders in pounding out the same number of pushups as our team's total score. When I liked a student's artwork at Senior Portfolio Night, I let him know and told him what I liked about it. Whether they're football players or artists, high school kids often don't want to let on that they care what you're saying and doing, but I have no doubt they do.

Just like aloof principals, a leader who doesn't convey a passion for the success of her organization shouldn't expect others to care either. If a leader doesn't demonstrate that she sincerely cares about the people in his organization, there's no reason she should care about each other.

Caring, ultimately, is infectious. Students care more about their homework when teachers show that it's something of value. Employees are more engaged when it's obvious that their leaders care.

CHALLENGE THE STATUS QUO

> "It's easy to confuse 'what is' with 'what ought to be,'
> especially when 'what is' has worked out in your favor."
> -Tyrion Lannister, *Game of Thrones*

"Periodically in the life of any organization," I said to the faculty members gathered in the high school's auditorium, "we need to take stock of our assumptions and reflect on our espoused values."

I had been principal of the school for five years and decided it was time to challenge their thinking about some collective decisions that shaped the work experiences of our newest teachers.

I continued by sharing this data:

- At that time, outside of specialized departments like physical education, 20% of teachers (about 35-40) taught in three different classrooms.
- Ten teachers taught in four different classrooms.
- Two taught in *five* different classrooms.
- Out of all those teachers who were frequently on the move, two-thirds were in their first three years of teaching.
- In one department, the situation was egregious. Six teachers taught in four or five classrooms, while 14 taught in only one. The six were among the least experienced in the department.

The conclusion was unmistakable. The data I shared was confounding evidence to the prevailing belief that we treated new teachers extremely well.

Having taught in multiple classrooms as a novice teacher myself – my maximum was three in a given day – I knew how those transitions took time and energy away from teaching. Transporting materials and making sure technology worked took limited time away for bathroom breaks or getting organized for your next class. By asking novices instead of more experienced teachers to deal with this substantial inconvenience, we weren't setting them up for success. We weren't "talking the talk and walking the walk."

As my brief presentation to the faculty continued, I explained that I was "not pointing fingers." The circumstances that I described resulted from "decisions based on assumptions that the school has lived with for years." However, that didn't mean we couldn't fix it. Then I expressed my hope that we do better. Because classroom assignments are departmental decisions, I directed supervisors to grapple with the question at their next department meeting.

As classroom assignments were completed that spring, I noted we had made good progress. Veteran teachers were sharing more of the burden of switching classrooms. Seniority was no longer the sole determinant of who got the most favorable classroom assignments. The solutions that each department identified may not have gone as far as I had hoped, but we were closer to "walking the walk."

Successful leaders dare to challenge, in Tyrion Lannister's words, "what is." They take stock of assumptions and ensure that the organization reflects on espoused values. When it's called for, leaders must challenge the current order and make changes – even turn things upside down if that's what's needed.

Restauranteur Danny Meyer, Founder and CEO of the tremendously successful Union Square Hospitality Group, sees this willingness to question the most fundamental assumptions of an organization as part of his company's "servant leadership" culture. Meyer explains that leaders need to

> ". . . basically flip the classic work chart and [then] let gravity work. If I'm the CEO of the company, instead of being the top of the pyramid, I'm actually at the bottom. The pyramid is flipped upside down. All accountability rests with me, but my primary job is to serve the people who I'm asking to serve our customers, who will then be responsible for serving their communities and our suppliers and, ultimately, our investors."

Meyer wasn't just talking. He controversially embraced this approach when he eliminated tipping at many of his restaurants. At top-level restaurants like Meyer's, tipping provides high compensation for servers, while leaving line cooks and other employees behind. In place of tipping, Meyer's restaurants raised menu prices – 20% or more in some restaurants – and commensurately raised wages of those employees who didn't benefit from tipping. According to Meyer's Union Square Hospitality Group, the "Hospitality Included" approach "is designed to compensate the entire team – in both the kitchen and the dining room – more equitably, competitively, and professionally." While Meyer's experiment remains unproven (some former employees claim it has increased turnover among servers), wages among many employees have increased, and profits reportedly remain stable.

Another successful organization, New Zealand's men's national rugby team, also employs this "upside down" approach in one of its traditions. Known as the All Blacks, the team doesn't delegate the job of "sweeping the sheds" (or locker room) to an equipment manager or new member of the team. Instead, the senior members of the squad assume this responsibility. Not even the best performers on the team are exempt from the small tasks that need to get done. This approach reinforces that the leaders of the team are there to serve. Retired All Blacks star Andrew Mehrtens, explains the humbling significance of sweeping the sheds: "It's not expecting somebody else to do your job for you. It teaches you not to expect things to be handed to you."

I tried, from time to time, to convey a similar message for staff members in our school. A few times during my tenure, I drew the name of a faculty member from a hat and gave him or her a vacation day, and I served as the winning teacher's substitute. I managed to perform somewhat capably as a biology and a Special Education teacher, but was barely competent when I was "Teacher for a Day" for an advanced math instructor. Those experiences reminded me how mentally and physically demanding a day of teaching could be.

Truly inverting the pyramid as Danny Meyer proposed also means that a leader must first attend to the least powerful in his organization. Great leaders know that if the least powerful, least influential members of an organization are poorly treated – if their ideas and suggestions are readily dismissed – then it's quite likely there are unhealthy dynamics elsewhere in the organization. They also realize that if the powerless in an organization – like Danny Meyer's line cooks and coat checkers – are well treated, then the climate for all employees is likely to be positive. Successful organizations, in the long run, are healthy from the bottom up.

While visiting one high school in Minnesota a number of years ago, it was obvious that administrators there hadn't learned this lesson. As I stepped foot in the school building, which clearly had more than a few bells and whistles, I couldn't help but be impressed. My tour guide showed me the comfortable student commons, state-of-the-art science labs, and, just across from the main entrance, the hockey arena! (Hockey is both sport and religion in Minnesota, and a few of the most affluent school districts have their own rinks.)

Toward the end of the tour, my guide led me toward a lower level corridor with less exterior light in the rear of the building. It was there where the special education classes were held. I'm sure there were many kind teachers serving children well in that wing, but the relegation of disabled children to a back hallway stood in stark contrast to the gleaming, new hockey rink by the front entrance. I sense that if I peeled back the layers of that school, I would learn a lot about priorities and power.

Even before I arrived at SBHS, ensuring that students who could easily be marginalized in other schools had a place at the table was a priority. Marilyn Pruce, who served as Special Education Supervisor during my tenure, had a strong staff of teachers who vocally advocated for their students. Their classrooms were located throughout the school building, including one classroom for multiply-disabled students just a few steps from my office. Similarly, Sue Coyle, who held several supervisory roles at the high school, was a strong advocate for students who faced mental health and addiction problems. Marilyn and Sue's advocacy, along with a strong culture of inclusion, resulted in a humane and supportive environment for all kinds of kids.

Even at a school that values inclusion and diversity like SBHS, the springtime rituals of high school can be a difficult time for students who feel like they don't fit powerful social norms. Fortunately, a number of staff members worked hard to ensure that our proms reflected our inclusive values.

In one of my proudest moments as a principal, a gender-fluid student who identified as a male through most of high school attended prom in a dress and looked amazing. The student came to the event with a number of friends, and I kept an eye on their table all night to make sure other students were respectful. But there really was no need. The evening went flawlessly, and as I watched students depart outside the venue, the student chattered away.

"Have a good time?" I asked.

"I had a *great* time! I'm soooo tired from dancing. What about you?"

"I had a great time, too. Didn't you see me dancing!?" I responded, and we laughed. Everyone had a place at the table that night.

Daring leaders, exercising their empathy, challenge the status quo and the hierarchies that support it. They ensure that organizations are inclusive and attend to the least powerful. They are able to place themselves through empathy and imagination in the position of a line cook, a transgender student, or the employee who empties the wastebaskets. Through their eyes, the leader can gain a fuller view of the enacted values of an organization. When they don't like what they see, they act quickly to change it

Authority and autonomy. Daring to challenge the traditional hierarchies of organizations is also about a leader's willingness to give up authority and control in the right ways. Borrowing language from institutional theory's take on "loosely-coupled organizations," I often thought about "tight" and "loose" approaches to leadership. Effective leaders seek expand autonomy and minimize the number of areas where they have to exercise "tight" leadership. If leaders have to be hands-on in too many areas, it probably points to talent problems in those areas. I can think of many areas where I could exercise more loose oversight as a principal because of strong leadership.

A significant reason SBHS was named a National School of Character in 2011 is because of the leadership of Gina Welsh, who then served as Activities Director of the school. Gina coordinated the efforts of student and teacher leaders to take our character education initiatives from "good to great." She was also an excellent operational leader. She somehow managed, for example, to take dozens of teenagers (and her principal) on ski trips to Vermont and Park City, Utah and return them to school entirely intact.

Because I knew her to be trustworthy and responsible, I gave Gina a considerable degree of autonomy. We would discuss major issues, make decisions together, and then I'd stay out of her way.

Student Council fell under Gina's oversight, and their success continues to be a reflection of her effectiveness in mentoring outstanding advisors like Lauren Morris and Kelly Boyer. The SBHS Student Council, consistently rated among the best in the state, and the larger Student Senate are exemplary student organizations that accomplish a lot every year.

I'm certain that many leaders have moments when they pause and just enjoy all the good work that's happening around them. Gina and Lauren provided a number of those moments during my eight years as principal. I remember one such moment at my last pep rally as principal.

Several months before, Ian Moritz, the Student Council president at the time, had the audacious idea of earning himself and the student body a spot in the *Guinness Book of World Records*. Such an effort is actually a considerable logistical challenge when done right, but that didn't deter Ian. I stayed out of the way of people I trusted – Gina, Lauren, and Ian – and the planning for the rally where the record would be set moved forward.

Once the big event started I got to appreciate what a great team can accomplish. As the rally progressed, it was obvious that Ian would get his record with the help of many of his schoolmates. On March 16, 2012, Ian set the Guinness record for the most high-fives in an hour: 1,739.[19] At the end of the pep rally, as I thought about leaving the school, I knew that *this* rally was a perfect bookend to my "Back in Black" performance in my first year. I was quite happy to be out of the spotlight and let Ian and his team do their thing.

DEFY EXPECTATIONS

In the course of my leadership career, I've been fortunate to work with many individuals like Gina, Lauren, and Kelly who truly believe in the mission of the organization. They have rejected the more typical transactional model of organizations. In the for-profit world, for example, employment is a transaction between employees performing job responsibilities and the company that rewards them with compensation. In a transactional model of education, when students attend school regularly and behave themselves, they are rewarded with good grades.

More interesting to Debra Meyerson, then a professor at Stanford Business School, were those individuals in organizations who didn't follow the typical transactional pattern. Meyerson coined the term "tempered radical" for those individuals who see things differently from the norm, and, despite those differences, still want to achieve success for themselves and for their organizations.

Building from research involving hundreds of leaders, Meyerson identified a number of characteristics of the tempered

---

[19] Ian's record has since been toppled. As of publication, the record holder is Vickrant Mahajan of Jammu, India with 2,514. Congratulations, Vickrant.

radical. Tempered radicals see their unique perspectives as a strength that can be an impetus for change. They believe direct, angry confrontation will get them nowhere, but they aren't passive either. They take on problems and don't allow frustrations with the status quo to fester.

Tempered radicals, according to Meyerson, "work quietly to challenge prevailing wisdom and gently provoke their organizational cultures to adapt." Ultimately, they seek to bring about significant change through approaches we might consider modest and unassuming. They defy expectations by using their relationships, the power of their ideas, and their ability to communicate to get important results.

Like those quiet, diligent tempered radicals, it's easy to miss those people who defy expectations in a significant, but unassuming way. Absorbed in my own world on a Saturday night in a Best Buy store, I almost missed one of those moments.

About a decade ago, I was running errands and decided to make a quick stop to buy a new cell phone case. As inevitably happens to me at Best Buy, I was soon drawn to other shiny expensive objects. This was the heyday of the iPod, and I was, in particular, admiring a slim gold one that was about the third of the size of MP3 player I used at the gym.

Next to me perusing the same devices were a father and son. Dad was a tallish, bearded man in a Carhartt jacket and sturdy work boots. His son looked like a typical nine-year-old, visibly excited as he carefully reviewed his iPod options.

"You don't have enough birthday money for that one, but I'll add a little extra so you can get it."

The boy beamed up at his father, excitedly nodded, and continued to look over the electronics display.

After a few minutes passed, the father said a bit impatiently, "Alright, that's enough looking. We need to get going. Mom's waiting. What color do you want?"

The boy looked up at his dad, then glanced back at one particular iPod, then looked up again at his dad just a bit hesitantly.

"The pink one."

The father paused long enough for a deep breath, his face clearly belying the many thoughts racing through his head.

Standing next to them, trying to act like the casual shopper, I couldn't help but hold my own breath, eager to see how the scene played out.

"You sure you want the pink one?" he said.

The boy nodded.

Pause.

"OK, get it and let's go."

Sometimes the most daring gestures are small ones. Sometimes those we least expect to defy expectations do it in a most meaningful way.

To this day, I wonder how that father and son – both of whom dared to be different – are getting along. I suspect very well.

CHAPTER TEN

BRICK BY BRICK

I left my comfortable apartment on a chilly, cloudless Sunday morning to head to my office to write these very words. Except for a few city dwellers walking their dogs, the streets of Center City Philadelphia were empty.

I turned left onto JFK Boulevard as the sun, low on the horizon, blinded me for a moment. After walking a couple of blocks, I noticed a line of men, bundled up, waiting patiently in line for something – perhaps the elevator down to the subway? I knew this path well. On most days, it was bustling with people hurrying from Point A to Point B. But this time there was this incongruous line outside an office building.

I got within a block of the line and noticed a man peel away from the line carrying a clear plastic bag in hand. The rest of the men, all of them disheveled in some way, shifted from foot to foot, many looked down at their feet. Few if any talked.

The next man in line then stepped toward a card table tended by a volunteer. The table was covered in bags filled with sandwiches, apples, bananas, napkins.

The line crossed the width of the sidewalk, and as I approached, a man with a scraggly beard took a half step back to let me through as I said a quiet "Excuse me."

A block further on, I crossed a large concrete plaza across from City Hall. A few yards away, a man in a wheelchair pushed himself around, looking in the windows of stores and offices that surrounded the square. Near him was a large pile of boxes and a blue Ikea bag filled with papers and other things that probably insulated him from the cold the evening before. A lyric from a favorite song crossed my mind: "Out of our night of struggle." I crossed the street and walked the final block to my office.

Settled into place, I sat down to write, still thinking of the dozen men in tattered coats waiting for sandwiches. When the words didn't flow, I launched Spotify and played the song that had come to my mind in the plaza.

Out of the ruins and rubble
Out of the smoke
Out of our night of struggle
Can we see a ray of hope?

As Hunter Parrish sang "Beautiful City" from *Godspell*, I thought about all the challenges to optimism in our world in early 2018. School shootings, serial bombings, war in Syria, demagoguery that tries to pass as leadership. And the lonely man pushing himself around the plaza in his wheelchair. Rays of hope were elusive in that moment.

. . . We can start
Slowly but surely mending
Brick by brick
Heart by heart
Now, maybe now
We start learning how

When the words didn't flow, I paused to review a few notes for another chapter of this book. I was reminded of the late Admiral Jim Stockdale, spending years behind the bars of the brutal "Hanoi Hilton" prison during the Vietnam War. He didn't give up despite having every reason to do so. Stockdale, as I described in Chapter 5, found ways to help his fellow prisoners survive brutality and   isolation.

When your trust is all but shattered
When your faith is all but killed
You can give up bitter and battered
Or you can slowly start to build

His mind battered and limbs shattered by torture, Stockdale retained a rational optimism that strengthened the resolve of the prisoners. Step by step, he built a brotherhood that enabled them to survive.

Like Stockdale and other leaders in seemingly hopeless situations, we are left with an important choice. Battered and bruised by the challenges we face, we can disengage and accept our fate, or we can try to find a way forward.

The song concludes,

> *A Beautiful City*
> *Yes, we can.*
> *We can build a beautiful city*
> *Not a city of angels*
> *But finally a city of man*

It's up to us, not the angels, to build this "beautiful city." What's your beautiful city? Is it . . .

A loving and respectful family?
A successful non-profit that meets feeds and comforts our most vulnerable citizens?
A character-driven team that gets results?
An ethical, ambitious company that honors the contributions of its employees?
A school that unleashes the brilliant potential of its students?

As we do the hard work to build families, companies, teams, and schools worthy of admiration, it's tempting to give up when we read discouraging headlines. Despite the blows dealt to the notion of leadership by unethical executives and self-absorbed politicians, I remain optimistic. I know too many good people – a number of whom are described in these pages – who aspire to make a difference. They are imaginative, authentic leaders who have the strength to persevere. Inspired by their examples, we have every reason to press on. We must move forward, step by step, brick by brick, heart by heart.

Admiral Stockdale had every reason to give up. He survived, he said, because in the end,

"I never lost faith in the end of the story."

Neither have I.

ACKNOWLEDGMENTS
AND REFERENCES

Many good people helped contributed to *Leadership that Lasts*. I'm fortunate to have family and friends who have generously contributed moral support through this writing journey.

I specifically want to thank nine people who provided feedback on specific chapters of the book: Jay Barth, Carl Blanchard, Elizabeth Bornstein, Kristen Brown, Scott Hinckley, Michael Miller, Jocelyn Pickford, Peter Shulman, and my nephew, Evan Matheney. Their encouragement and feedback made this a better book. I'm particularly indebted to Carl for his assistance in reworking a problematic chapter.

In addition, I'm grateful for two individuals who served as primary editors for the book. First, April Gonzalez is a wonderful friend, great leader, and fantastic principal. Fortunately for me, April was also an outstanding AP English teacher for many years!

I cannot adequately thank my other major editor and my greatest love, Kendric Chua. Ken unfailingly supports my dreams, no matter how crazy. He put up with me through caffeine-fueled weeks of writing. No one was more integral to the creation of this book. He designed the book's amazing cover and was particularly helpful in shaping the personal stories I shared. Love you, Ken.

I also very appreciative of two groups of educators who have inspired and informed my thinking about leadership. First, I'm grateful for a number of leaders, past and present, of South Brunswick High School. Peter Varela, Susana Nikitczuk, Jaymee Boehmer, Sue Coyle, Yoshi Donato, Pat Abitabilo, Gina Welsh, Elaine McGrath and many others – I could fill pages with their names – who contributed so much to our work together. I particularly want to thank Dr. Gary McCartney, the former Superintendent of the South Brunswick School District, for taking a chance in hiring a young, idealistic principal from the Midwest in

2004. Gary shared many lessons of leadership when we worked together, and a number of them are reflected in this book.

Finally, I would like to thank the 62 Philadelphia principals who were a part of the Neubauer Fellowship in Educational Leadership when I served as Executive Director of the Philadelphia Academy of School Leaders. They continue to inspire me with their desire to go the extra mile to serve the children of our city.

REFERENCES

Chapter 3: **CONNECT**
    Significance: *Man's Search for Meaning* by Victor Frankl. choirchoirchoir.com. davidbyrne.com/journal/how-do-they-do-it-part-2. *Setting the Table: The Transforming Power of Hospitality in Business* by Danny Meyer. www.forbes.com/sites/micahsolomon/2015/05/04/restaurant-magnate-danny-meyer-on-customer-service-leadership-and-the-right-way-to-be-greedy/#199260cb2558.
    Traditional communication: *All the Best, George Bush: My Life in Letters and Other Writings* by George H.W. Bush. www.nytimes.com/2017/01/20/us/politics/letters-from-presidents-to-successors.html.

Chapter 4: **COMMIT**
    Introduction: www1.gmnews.com/2008/10/23/former-sbhs-teacher-faces-three-years-in-prison.
    Losing your way: aviationknowledge.wikidot.com/aviation:60-to-1-rule.
    Commitments and pledges: www.usatoday.com/story/news/nation/2013/11/15/fraternity-pledge-hazing-death/3584501. www.hanknuwer.com/hazing-deaths._sam.org/fraternity/about-us. beta.org/about/about-beta-theta-pi. *True Gentlemen: The Broken Pledge of America's Fraternities* by John Hechinger. www.nj.com/middlesex/index.ssf/2014/10/rutgers_student_caitlyn_kovacs_died_of_alcohol_poisoning_after_party_autopsy_finds.html. www.theatlantic.com/magazine/archive/2017/11/a-death-at-penn-state/540657.
    Enacting values: www.mycentraljersey.com/story/news/local/middlesex-county/2015/01/01/sisterhood-traveling-prom-dresss/21119107.
    Alignment: www.cnbc.com/2016/12/02/13-inspiring-quotes-on-leadership-and-success-from-starbucks-ceo-howard-schultz.html. markets.businessinsider.com/news/stocks/starbucks-builds-on-its-foundation-of-industry-leading-benefits-for-retail-employees-announcing-new-investments-in-comprehensive-paid-leave-and-wage-1013838216.
    Orientation and re-orientation: *The Art of Fielding* by Chad Herbach, p. 503.
    Show your commitment: si.com/mmqb/2017/01/25/nfl-bill-belichick-new-england-patriots-naval-academy-super-bowl-li. www.nytimes.com/2017/08/01/us/politics/coast-guard-commandant-general-zukunft-transgender-troops.html.

He showed up: www.youtube.com/watch?v=BtJJViD_IIh8.
www.newsweek.com/five-who-survived-144813. maninredbandana.com.
www.nytimes.com/2002/05/26/nyregion/fighting-to-live-as-the-towers-died.html.

Chapter 5: **PERSEVERE**
Introduction: *A Farewell to Arms* by Ernest Hemingway, Chapter 34.
Volatile and uncertain:
www.washingtonpost.com/archive/local/1995/12/02/gen-maxwell-r-thurman-dies-at-64/5542cc8d-cadc-4e13-b988-e278296e24bb/?utm_term=.b191c0d2ebb3.
www.dtic.mil/dtic/tr/fulltext/u2/a251129.pdf. www.thoughtco.com/life-is-suffering-what-does-that-mean-450094.
Denial: news.harvard.edu/gazette/story/2008/06/text-of-j-k-rowling-speech.
One step at a time: www.youtube.com/watch?v=RKvRvrF56gI.
www.pgatour.com/news/2008/djblog.html. *Walking with Friends: An Inspirational Year on the PGA Tour* by D.J. Gregory and Steve Eubanks.
video.londonbusinessforum.com/detail/videos/inspire-me/video/5211135043001/sir-dave-brailsford---the-1-factor?autoStart=true.
www.njleg.state.nj.us/2012/Bills/PL12/26_.PDF.
Mantras: www.sportingnews.com/nfl/news/2017-super-bowl-51-li-patriots-bill-belichick-do-your-job-tom-brady-matthew-slater/a0x7dcnkgk910ktfvztgvyno. "Follow Me," unpublished manuscript, by Dennis S. Matheney. www.nytimes.com/1994/01/22/obituaries/aubrey-s-newman-90-colonel-famed-for-follow-me-battle-cry.html.
www.washingtonpost.com/blogs/answer-sheet/post/steve-jobs-told-students-stay-hungry-stay-foolish/2011/10/05/gIQA1qVjOL_blog.html?utm_term=.58271727bcb6.
www.npr.org/templates/story/story.php?storyId=94658913.
Rituals: www.allblacks.com/Teams/Haka. *Power of Myth* with Bill Moyers and Joseph Campbell.
Long walks and long goodbyes: *Long Walk to Freedom: The Autobiography of Nelson Mandela* by Nelson Mandela.

Chapter 6: **THRIVE**
Introduction: www.youtube.com/watch?v=1LKJ5ZzzL0wgb13k. Quote widely attributed to Gandhi including *Stress Management for Life: A Research-Based Experiential Approach* by Michael Olpin and Margie Hesson.
Authenticity: "A Poet's Advice to Students" from *E. E. Cummings: A Miscellany* edited by George Firmage. *Dr. Zhivago* by Boris Pasternak, "Conclusion."
Vulnerability: postsecret.com. www.humansofnewyork.com.
"Close to the Core": minimalismfilm.com. www.theminimalists.com/288. lifeedited.com. *Flow: The Psychology of Optimal Experience* by Mihaly Csíkszentmihályi.

Chapter 7: **DISCOVER**
Humility: *The Road to Character* by David Brooks, Chapter 1.
www.inc.com/empact/bill-gates-warren-buffett-and-oprah-all-use-the-5-hour-rule.html.

Curiosity: *Drama High: The Incredible True Story of a Brilliant Teacher, a Struggling Town, and the Magic of Theater* by Michael Sokolove, pp. 97-99. *The Seven Habits of Highly Effective People: Powerful Lessons in Personal Change*, pp. 236-245.
Design thinking: dschool.stanford.edu.
www.theatlantic.com/magazine/archive/2017/01/what-makes-things-cool/508772.
www.ted.com/talks/jeanne_gang_buildings_that_blend_nature_and_city#t-19585.
Improvement science:
www.ihi.org/resources/Pages/HowtoImprove/ScienceofImprovementEstablishingMeasures.aspx. www.carnegiefoundation.org/blog/improvement-is-a-team-sport.
The first "O": www.artofmanliness.com/2014/09/15/ooda-loop. dnipogo.org/john-r-boyd.
www.theatlantic.com/notes/2015/08/john-boyd-in-the-news-all-you-need-to-know-about-ooda-loop/402847.
www.theatlantic.com/national/archive/2014/03/john-boyd-from-em-us-news-em/284223.
MBWA: www.leadership-central.com/situational-leadership-theory.html#axzz5Bp1NJQ3L. *School Leadership that Works: From Research to Results* by Robert Marzano, Timothy Waters, and Brian A. McNulty, Chapter 4.
Questioning: *The Innovator's DNA: Mastering the Five Skills of Disruptive Innovators* by Jeffrey Dyer, Hal Gregersen, and Clayton Christensen, Chapters 1 and 3. hbr.org/2013/07/catalytic-questioning-five-ste. *Legacy: What the All Blacks Can Teach Us About the Business of Life* by James Kerr, Chapter 1. *Whatever It Takes: How Professional Learning Communities Respond When Kids Don't Learn* by Richard DuFour, Rebecca DuFour, Robert Eaker, and Gayle Karhanek, "Introduction".
More and better: godinallthings.com/2013/03/11/magis.
Twitter.com/JamesMartinSJ/status/926964931232239616.

Chapter 8: **IMAGINE**
Introduction: character.org/schools-of-character/national-schools-of-character-overview/national-schools-of-character/winners/2011-national-schools-of-character/2011-national-schools-of-character/south-brunswick-high-school.
When imagination fails.
govinfo.library.unt.edu/911/report/911Report.pdf.
I-M-P-U-T-E?: *Steve Jobs* by Walter Isaacson, p. 78.
Re-imagining: harvard.edu/gazette/story/2008/06/text-of-j-k-rowling-speech.
Re-imagining leadership development: phillyschoolleaders.org.
Re-imagining entertainment: *Cirque Du Soleil: 20 Years Under the Sun - An Authorized History* by Tony Babinski and Kristian Manchester. www.cirquedusoleil.com/about/history.
Re-imagining the chorus: schools.nyc.gov/OA/SchoolReports/2016-17/School_Quality_Snapshot_2017_EMS_R022.pdf.
www.youtube.com/channel/UC19wHqb_vnglAFaFF3a7DNA.
www.youtube.com/user/NJPictures.
Faith, hope and realism: *Good to Great: Why Some Companies Make the Leap While Others Don't* by Jim Collins., pp. 83-87.

Excellence: sethgodin.typepad.com. *Daniel H. Burnham, Architect, Planner of Cities. Volume 2* by Charles Moore, Chapter 25.

Imagination and stewardship: *Legacy: What the All Blacks Can Teach Us About the Business of Life* by James Kerr, Chapter 14.

Chapter 9: **DARE**

Introduction: "Back in Black" from *Back in Black* by Brian Johnson, Angus Young, and Malcolm Young.

Leading with audacity: *Built to Last: Successful Habits of Visionary Companies* by Jim Collins and Jerry Porras. *Good to Great: Why Some Companies Make the Leap While Others Don't* by Jim Collins, Chapter 9.
www.nj.com/education/2015/03/parcc_starts_nj.html.

Find your own path: www.youtube.com/watch?v=oBm100trLLU.

Challenge the status quo: blueprint.cbre.com/danny-meyer-a-restaurant-empire-built-on-hospitality. www.grubstreet.com/2017/10/danny-meyer-no-tips-staff-expectations.html. www.ushgnyc.com/hospitalityincluded. *Legacy: What the All Blacks Can Teach Us About the Business of Life* by James Kerr, Chapter 1. patch.com/new-jersey/southbrunswick/south-brunswick-high-school-breaks-guinness-world-record.

Defy expectations: hbr.org/2001/10/radical-change-the-quiet-way. *Tempered Radicals: How People Use Difference to Inspire Change at Work* by Debra E. Meyerson.

Chapter 10: **BRICK BY BRICK**

"Beautiful City" from *Godspell* by Stephen Schwartz. *Good to Great: Why Some Companies Make the Leap While Others Don't* by Jim Collins, pp. 83-85.

*The beautiful cover photograph was taken
by pixabay.com member Couleur.*